Library of Congress Cataloging-in-Publication Data is available.

ISBN 978-1-5235-1048-1

Design by Becky Terhune
Cover and interior photography by Penny De Los Santos
Food and prop stylist: Judy Haubert
Photo credits: **Shutterstock.com**: Francesco Carniani p. viii; Natallia Novik p. 1; Sobakapavlova p. 71; Homydesignz p. 91; bekulnis p. 109; Sokol Artstudio p. 133.

Workman books are available at special discounts when purchased in bulk for premiums and sales promotions as well as for fundraising or educational use. Special editions or book excerpts can also be created to specification. For details, contact the Special Sales Director at specialmarkets@workman.com.

Workman Publishing Co., Inc.
225 Varick Street
New York, NY 10014-4381
workman.com

WORKMAN is a registered trademark of Workman Publishing Co., Inc.

Printed in the United States of America
First printing November 2021

10 9 8 7 6 5 4 3 2 1

CONTENTS

NACHOS! FOR DINNER?!?

How many times have you gone out to dinner and gotten nachos as an appetizer and then not been that hungry for your main meal? Or even worse—*not* gotten nachos thinking it would be too much?! Nachos are one of those appetizers that are usually just a little too big to be a true app, and a little too small and imbalanced to be dinner.

Not anymore! Once I realized that you could have nachos for dinner, it was like the key unlocking the vault of nacho secrets.

You may be wondering: What makes nachos for dinner different from nachos as an appetizer or a bar snack? One word: balance.

I talk a lot about balance in these recipes, whether it is balancing textures, flavors, temperatures, or even colors. But the balance I am referring to here has more to do with balancing the typical requirements of dinner—nutrition, satiety, equal representation of the "food groups"—with the big flavors, varied textures, and fun offered by a plate of nachos. Look, we all love over-the-top loaded nachos, and there are plenty of those in these pages, but when nachos deliver protein and veggies with a little less cheese on the chip (and when "chip" can mean more than tortillas), they become more acceptable as a dinner instead of being relegated to Snackville.

Using hearty toppings and building nachos around classic dinner dishes, these are recipes you can serve for dinner to family and friends, whether it be for a quick weeknight meal or an epic Sunday night feast. Yes, most of these nachos are a complete meal in and of themselves. But I'm not saying this is diet food. They range from pretty healthy (as far as nachos are concerned) to indulgent comfort food.

I tried to incorporate as many veggies as possible and provide vegan swap-outs. I wanted these recipes to be accessible, and to be honest, some of the best nachos I have ever had were vegan (shout-out to Taco Party in Somerville, Massachusetts!).

I thought it would be fun to organize this collection like a traditional cookbook, with nachos based on appetizers, salads, sandwiches, hearty dinners, and more. So you'll find everything from spinach artichoke nachos and caprese nachos to cheeseburger nachos and even dessert'chos like apple pie nachos! The flavors and ingredients of these dishes range from the classic (including a nod to the first known nacho recipe; see below) to the boundary-pushing (Chicken Larb Nachos on page 85) to the totally outrageous (Chicken and Waffle Nachos on page 137).

A BRIEF HISTORY OF NACHOS

Before we can talk about nachos, we have to begin with the corn tortilla. Corn tortillas were developed by the Maya thousands of years ago. They soaked hard, inedible corn kernels in limewater (also called pickling lime) to remove the skin and soften the kernels, then ground them into masa flour, which they turned into dough, thus making the creation of the tortilla possible. (It was during the Spanish conquest of the Maya that these corn cakes took their current name, tortillas, meaning "little cakes" in Spanish.)

But frying the tortillas to make them crispy predates the Spanish invasion. The dish chilaquiles—comprised of fried tortillas tossed in a chile sauce—dates all the way back to the Aztecs; the name itself is from the Aztec Nahuatl language and means "chiles and greens." Take a *big* leap forward to the 1940s, and the modern nacho is born—in Piedras Negras, Coahuila, Mexico, a city on the Rio Grande, right over the US border from the Texas town of Eagle Pass. Eagle Pass was home to a large American army base, Fort Duncan, and because of the base's proximity to the border, many off-duty soldiers and their families would cross the bridge to get their first glimpse of Mexican culture.

As the story goes, Ignacio Anaya—known familiarly as Nacho—was working as the maître d' of a restaurant called the Victory Club when twelve army wives came in for a snack. It was off hours at the restaurant, so there was no chef on duty at the time. Wanting to welcome his customers regardless of the hour or lack of staff, Nacho went into the kitchen to see what he could make.

He fried up some tortillas, topped them with cheese, put them under the broiler, then added slices of jalapeño. He was debating what to call his creation when—according to one account—a guest said, "How about Nacho's special?" Well, the name stuck and the dish was a hit. A recipe for nachos was featured in a community cookbook as early as 1950, and when processed cheese was invented in the 1970s, nachos became a sports stadium favorite.

Today, you can find nachos as an appetizer at most chain restaurants and sports bars across the United States. In the dish's birthplace, the city of Piedras Negras, there's even the annual International Nacho Festival, featuring live music and a world's biggest nacho contest. In recent years, the fest has drawn more than 25,000 attendees to celebrate Nacho's creation and the legend it has become.

MY NACHO JOURNEY

As was the case for so many American kids who grew up in the late 1980s and early '90s, nachos were the first dish I ever learned to make by myself. My after-school recipe started with "restaurant style" chips on a paper plate. (Why are those chips even a thing? They are way too big to eat or dip properly.) I used American cheese (from the deli, not prewrapped singles—I'm not an animal!) or "Mexican blend" if I was lucky and my mom had picked it up at the store. I'd put a bunch of cheese on the chips—always careful not to overdo it—and microwave them until the cheese was melted in some areas and burnt, bubbly, and dried out in others. I served my nachos with Pace salsa; I preferred the thin kind when I was younger, later graduating to the thick and chunky stuff.

Fast-forward a few years to my parents' kitchen, where I'd regularly whip up nachos after a night out. My friends would stumble into the basement while I'd drunkenly assemble nachos on a sheet pan, sure I was being too quiet to wake my folks, then creep down the stairs with the hot pan fresh from the oven. Everyone always devoured them. One friend loved them so much that he even mentioned them in his speech at my wedding, crediting nachos as the catalyst for my culinary career.

Years later I was in the right place at the right time and ended up helping a guy open a burrito shop. Many people who know me well might say, "Don't you mean the wrong place at the wrong time?" But my three years at the burrito shop actually helped me learn so much about working in restaurants and even more about Tex-Mex cuisine. I was resistant to putting nachos on the menu because I wanted the place to operate as a well-oiled burrito machine, but when the owner surprised me with a Tornado oven (like a super-high-powered toaster) specifically for nachos, I had to oblige. The nachos were never a bestseller at the restaurant, but they did have a cult following. Many of the recipes I originally developed for that burrito shop can be found in these pages, like the Carnitas (page 50) and Pico de Gallo (page 14).

I want to make one thing very clear at the outset: I am a white man writing a book of recipes that riff conceptually (and sometimes materially) on Mexican dishes and also play with ideas derived from culinary traditions from all over the world. I have always tried to explore new flavors and tastes and learn about different cultures through food, which I have been writing about on my blog, *The Food in My Beard*, since 2008. I strive to appreciate and not appropriate, and I strongly believe that everyone should be able to cook whatever they want. That said, we have been separating the food from the culture for far too long in the food space, and that needs to stop. I am here to celebrate different cultures through food, not erase them; to explore and learn, not to steal or "upgrade." So I encourage you to look at the ideas presented in these pages as fun, creative dinners and not as authentic representations of any particular cuisine. If you end up loving the flavors in, say, the Chicken Tikka Masala Naanchos on page 114 or the Braised Lamb Beerbacoa on page 56, then I hope you'll take the next step and dig into cookbooks written by authors from those particular cultures; their varied perspectives and experiences will offer more authentic, well-rounded representations of the culinary traditions that have inspired me here.

SO WHAT ARE NACHOS?

At the pure base level, nachos consist of two or three ingredients: Tortilla chips. Melted cheese. Jalapeños (optional).

You could argue that the topping is necessary since the original plate of nachos was topped with jalapeños. But I bet there are millions of kids who put cheese on top of chips and microwave them until it gets melty, skipping jalapeños and other toppings altogether—and who am I to say those don't qualify? In my opinion, riffs on the dish pay homage to the spirit of the original, which was a "what can I put together to feed these people fast" situation. It was in that spirit of invention and creativity that I developed the recipes for this book. The dishes here range from pretty traditional to really far out, but they all include the Three Pillars of Nacho as established in Anaya's original special:

- Crispy base (chips)

- Melty layer (usually cheese)

- Flavorful topper (such as jalapeños)

ONCE YOU HAVE THE THREE PILLARS OF NACHO, THE WORLD IS YOUR NACHO PLATE.

In my book (which is *this* book), the crunchy base doesn't have to be tortilla chips. It doesn't have to be chips at all. Honestly, it doesn't even have to be handheld or hold the toppings on its own. I stuck with tortilla chips for most of these recipes so they still retain the true spirit of nachos, but occasionally things go off the rails (or off the chips, I guess).

The melty part doesn't have to be cheese—but it might be the most important player. This is the binder that brings your nachos to life. If you were to just throw dry toppings onto chips, they wouldn't really come together as true nachos. This layer has to be viscous enough to cling to the crunchy element. If the layer is too thin (or in the case of a sauce, too watery), it will not bind the "chips" properly and—even worse—might make them soggy. This is why, when I was a broke college kid, dumping a can of refried beans on top of a pile of chips *was* nachos (sad nachos, but nachos nonetheless), but dumping hot sauce on naked chips was *not*.

Toppings are arguably the least important element of nachos—you can omit toppings and *technically* you'll still have nachos—but they're where the true heart and soul of nachos come through. For me, an ideal plate of nachos has a topping with lots of umami, another with a little heat, and still another that's sour or pickled to form a perfect balance.

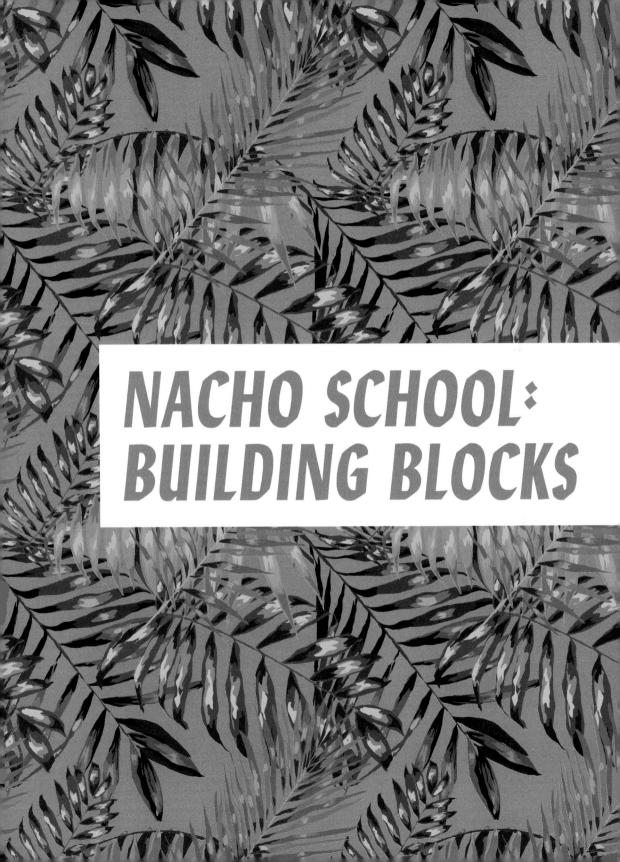

NACHO SCHOOL: BUILDING BLOCKS

THE FIVE SECRETS OF NACHO SUCCESS

When people see me making nachos they often ask, "Why are you being so meticulous? I wouldn't have the patience to do it like that for something as casual as nachos."

But here's the thing. It only takes maybe an extra three minutes to pay attention to the topping distribution, but it pays off so well in the end. We have all had *that* pile of nachos from a restaurant—where the uppermost chips are overloaded with cheese and toppings and the bottom ones are naked. Half of the chips get soggy within a few minutes, and you need to start being creative about how to redistribute the toppings as you eat.

That's why I make all of my nachos in a single layer and I encourage you to do the same. A sheet panful (technically, a half-sheet size, 18 x 13 inches) will serve as dinner for three or four people, or an appetizer for up to eight. Here are a few steps toward a successful nacho build:

1. Take an extra minute to move all the chips around on the pan. Spread them out so that every chip has at least 50 percent of its surface area exposed to the pan's surface. Leave no chip behind.

2. Sprinkle half of the cheese first, then the toppings, then the remaining cheese. This double-cheesing helps the toppings stick to the chips and also can keep the chips from getting soggy.

3. Cut everything up into small, equal-size pieces. This helps with even distribution and keeps everything bite-size and easy to pick up on a single chip.

4. Spread out the toppings. Okay, so for example, if you were making the Chicken Broccoli Alfredo Nachos on page 112, *no*, you wouldn't have to put a piece of chicken and a piece of broccoli on each individual chip. *But* as you sprinkle or dollop on your toppings, I'd urge you to be aware of where they're landing; when you are almost done, go back and fill in any empty areas. When I'm assembling nachos, I like to squint my eyes to assess the color distribution of each topping, almost as if the nachos are an abstract painting and I'm making sure the colors are represented uniformly. Does that make me a nacho artist? Who's to say?

5. To dip or to top. The perfectionist in me wants to spread the chips evenly with the cold toppings when they come out of the oven so that each chip delivers a perfectly calculated ratio of ingredients in every bite—but sometimes it is better to reserve the toppings on the side for dipping. This keeps the chips crispy and the nachos themselves less messy, and it lets the eaters decide how much salsa, sour cream, or other cold topping they want. The common restaurant method is to slap the guacamole and sour cream right in the center of the nacho pile, but this makes a mess and is a pain to eat, so I rarely do it this way.

DIFFERENT WAYS TO GIVE A CHIP

Thick, thin, and all sorts of different shapes: I love all chips, but some are better for nachos than others. For me the best nacho chip is triangular and can be eaten in one large bite.

HOMEMADE	Sturdy, thick, don't get soggy easily.
ARTISANAL/ AUTHENTIC	There are a few brands that hit pretty close to actual homemade, and they're worth seeking out if you're not going to make your own. They usually come in a brown paper bag with a little window. You shouldn't see too many broken chips through the window. Many grocery stores actually fry their leftover tortillas and sell them as chips, and this can also be a great option. I like Mi Niña and Donkey brand chips.
INDUSTRIAL	These are the chips you'll find in every supermarket and convenience store. They begin life not as a round tortilla but in triangular chip shape, just waiting to be fried. Their texture is almost grainy when compared to homemade, and they'll break easily and become soggy if you don't build your nachos correctly (see The Five Secrets of Nacho Success, page 2). Still, you can't beat them for availability and price. If you want to use industrial chips, try to find Late July or Mission, which are my favorites.
FLAVORED	These are the can't-stop-eating-them chips of your childhood (and/or adulthood), the ones dusted with irresistible chemically engineered flavor powder. Although I grew up eating them, I wouldn't normally make nachos with them—*unless* the chips' flavor matched the flavor profile of the dish or added a fun, unexpected twist.
COMPOSITION	Traditional tortilla chips are made with white or yellow corn, but you'll encounter other colors, too. Blue corn chips have been popular for a while, as have red and green (which get their color from natural or artificial dyes). You'll also find "tortilla" chips that are made with whole grains, beans, sweet potato, and other base ingredients instead of (or in addition to) corn. These chips wouldn't be my first choice for nacho making, but if I came up with an idea that really worked with one of them, I would go for it. The sweet potato chips from Food Should Taste Good are particularly good and work well with a black bean nacho or in place of the plantain chips in the Plantain Nachos on page 89.
SHAPED	I usually opt for small-ish triangular tortilla chips for nachos. You know, your standard chip. Some people like "restaurant style" chips, which are very wide triangles, but I think they're much too big to eat in one bite and they often break in the bag anyway. There are also round chips, oval chips, and of course, chip cups. The cups have their place; they do work for making individual nacho-style bites and are also great for dipping in a thick guacamole. But they don't really stack well and would be my last choice for nachos.

TORTILLA CHIPS

**MAKES 90 CHIPS
(ENOUGH FOR 1 BATCH
OF NACHOS)**
Takes about 15 minutes

Vegetable or peanut oil,
   for frying

15 corn tortillas
   (4 to 6 inches each)

Kosher salt

I will be the first to admit that I don't always make my own chips. There are a lot of great brands out there with quality chips that work well in nachos. (More on that on page 3.) But every time I do make my own, I wonder why I don't do it more often. The chips come out glistening with oil and salt, crispy, and especially sturdy—perfect for nachos. Plus, they don't get soggy the way many store-bought chips do, and they are pretty simple to make.

1 Pour the oil into a large, heavy-bottomed pot to a depth of 4 inches. Heat over medium-high heat until a deep-fry or candy thermometer inserted into the oil reaches 375°F. (If you do not have a thermometer, you can test the oil with a piece of tortilla. The oil should start bubbling around the edges of the tortilla right away, and it should get crispy in about 2 minutes. If it turns brown, the oil is too hot.) Set a cooling rack over a layer of paper towels.

2 While the oil comes up to temperature, stack the tortillas on a cutting board and cut them into 6 equal wedges. Separate the wedges.

3 Working in 3 or 4 batches, add the tortilla wedges to the hot oil. Fry the tortillas, stirring gently with a slotted spoon to ensure even browning and prevent them from sticking, until they are very crispy and starting to brown slightly (the bubbling of the oil will also begin to subside), 2 to 3 minutes. Use the slotted spoon to remove the chips from the oil and transfer them to the cooling rack. Let drain and and cool slightly.

4 Sprinkle the chips with a few generous pinches of salt. Toss the chips around a bit on the rack, then salt them again to season evenly.

5 Serve the chips immediately, or let them cool completely, then transfer them to a large ziplock bag with a paper towel inside to collect any moisture. The chips will keep at room temperature for up to 1 week (replace the paper towel every day).

Variation: The triangle is my default shape for homemade chips, but when you make your own, you can try any shape you want. Why not heart-shaped chips for a Valentine nacho? Stars on the Fourth of July? As long as the chips are roughly the size of a standard tortilla chip, the cook time should be the same as indicated.

NACHO CHEESE SAUCE

I have made a lot of cheese sauces in my day, especially when I was working on important tater tot research for my book *Tots!*, and there is nothing I love more than dumping a ton of cheese sauce over a plate of piping hot food. Some of my favorite nachos have cheese sauce, and some of the best ones have both melted cheese *and* sauce. After testing many, many cheese sauce recipes, I can't top this simple recipe, which I adapted from one made by J. Kenji López-Alt at Serious Eats. It's really tasty and pretty foolproof.

MAKES ABOUT 2 CUPS (ENOUGH FOR 1 BATCH OF NACHOS)

Takes about 15 minutes

1 can (12 ounces) evaporated milk

1 tablespoon cornstarch

2 cups (8 ounces) shredded cheddar cheese (see Note, page 9)

2 teaspoons hot sauce (see Note, page 11)

1 Whisk together the evaporated milk and cornstarch in a large frying pan to combine. Set the mixture over medium-high heat and bring it to a simmer, whisking often. Simmer, still whisking, until it thickens to the consistency of a thin chowder, about 1 minute. Remove from the heat.

2 Add the cheese and stir to incorporate. The cheese should melt into the sauce on the residual heat alone, but if it needs a little help, set the pan over low heat and cook, stirring, until the cheese melts completely, 3 to 5 minutes. Add the hot sauce and stir to combine.

3 Use immediately or store in a really good thermos; the sauce will stay warm for a few hours. Otherwise you can refrigerate it for up to 3 days and gently warm before serving.

NOTE: Shred the cheese directly from the block for this recipe. The pre-shredded stuff contains anticaking agents, meaning it won't melt into the creamy gooeyness you crave in a proper cheese sauce.

Variations

• Instead of the hot sauce, stir in 1 diced chipotle chile (canned in adobo) plus 1 teaspoon of adobo sauce from the can.

• Use a mix of cheeses, like cheddar and Jack, or even try replacing one-quarter of the cheese with feta or blue cheese.

• Stir some chopped chives and crumbled bacon into the finished sauce.

THE BIG CHEESE

I like to grate my own cheese for most recipes because it melts better than the shredded cheeses you can buy at the grocery store. That being said, many of the nachos in this book use a mix of cheddar and Jack cheeses; in those cases, a supermarket "Mexican blend" is a fine substitute for most nachos (just be aware that those industrial shredded cheeses are packaged with anticaking agents, which means they won't yield the kind of gooeyness you might typically associate with nachos).

I think using more than one cheese is usually better in any recipe, and nachos are no different. I choose my cheese based on what I want from it. When I do a cheddar and Jack mixture, then cheddar is there for flavor and Jack is for texture and meltability. You can see this same flavor and meltability combo in many of the recipes, especially when I use a cheese like blue cheese, Parmesan, or feta (none of which really melt well) and match it with Jack or mozzarella to give the nachos that oozy melty goodness that they need.

Cheese sauce is also common on nachos, and you'll find a great recipe on page 7 with some variations, plus a vegan option on page 10. When choosing to sauce or not to sauce, I let the recipe guide me. Obviously Cheesesteak Nachos on page 97 and Chicken Broccoli Alfredo Nachos on page 112 both need sauce, because sauce is a key component of the recipes that inspired them. I also use a sauce on nachos when I want to squeeze in another flavor, like in the Spicy 5-Pepper Nachos on page 126.

VEGAN "CHEESE" SAUCE

**MAKES ABOUT 2 CUPS
(ENOUGH FOR 1 BATCH
OF NACHOS)**

Takes about 20 minutes

⅓ cup solidified coconut oil

¼ cup diced yellow onion

¼ cup diced pickled
jalapeño (store-bought or
homemade; see page 29),
plus 1 tablespoon liquid
from the jar

1 clove garlic, peeled and
halved

½ cup peeled and diced Yukon
gold or russet potato

1 cup unsalted roasted cashews

½ cup oat milk or almond milk

1 teaspoon smoked paprika

1 tablespoon nutritional yeast

1 teaspoon hot sauce
(see Note)

For a few years, I lived across the street from a vegan taco shop, and their nachos were the best thing on the menu. I would go there for lunch all the time and get two tacos and nachos and be *so proud* of myself for eating vegan. The vegan cheese sauce on the nachos is what really makes them! And this one is awesome. I use coconut oil in this recipe because I like the flavor, but if you don't like it, you can use palm oil, which has a more neutral flavor, instead.

1 Melt the coconut oil in a large frying pan over medium heat.

2 Add the onion and jalapeño and cook, stirring occasionally, until softened, about 10 minutes. Add the garlic and cook for another 2 minutes or so, until the veggies are softened but haven't really started to brown on the edges.

3 Add the potatoes and cashews and lightly toast, about 3 minutes. Add the milk, ½ cup water, and paprika and bring to a simmer. Simmer until the potatoes are softened, about 10 minutes.

4 Transfer the mixture into a high-powered blender. Add the nutritional yeast, hot sauce, and jalapeño liquid. Turn the blender on high and blend until the mixture comes together to form a smooth sauce, about 5 minutes. If the mixture seems thick, add a splash of milk or water.

5 Use immediately or store in an airtight container in the fridge for up to 1 week. To reheat, microwave in 15-second increments, stirring in between and adding a little water if needed, until hot. Be careful not to overheat the sauce or it will separate (if that happens, you can bring it back together with the blender or hand blender).

NOTE: When it comes to hot sauce, the bottom line is to use your favorite! I usually have a few types on hand and switch which one I use depending on my mood. For a sauce like this, I often use something mild and vinegary like Frank's RedHot or Crystal, but sometimes I switch it up with another of my spicier favorites, Valentina.

VEGAN SUBSTITUTIONS

Even though my wife, Georgina, and I both love meat and cheese (and you'll see a lot of both in my Instagram feed), we actually try to eat vegan about 75 percent of the time. This is a goal we have set for our own health and the health of our planet, and I enjoy testing all the different vegan substitutions and replacement products out there.

When it comes to meat replacements, I love using Impossible Burger in place of any ground beef. In most heavily seasoned recipes that call for crumbled ground meat, it becomes hard to tell the difference. I have used this plant-based "meat" in the taco meat and chorizo recipes (see pages 49 and 54, respectively), and the results are almost identical to the meat versions. Gardein makes awesome breaded chicken and fish replacements (they're especially great when prepared in an air fryer) that would be perfect in the Chicken and Waffle Nachos (page 137) or Fish Taco Nachos (page 92).

When seeking a less processed replacement for shredded meats, I have used canned jackfruit and king oyster mushrooms to great success. Simply shred them, add some seasonings, and cook in oil over medium-high heat to crisp them up, then add sauce if desired.

As for vegan cheese options, I don't love the flavor or meltability of most of the store-bought vegan cheeses I have had, so I always opt for a vegan cheese sauce instead. Vegan nachos can be just as good as, if not better than, their cheesy and meaty counterparts, and the sauce is often where they live or die. I wanted to make sure you could adapt recipes in this book to vegan if needed, and by using the delicious vegan cheese sauce on page 10 and a variety of protein alternatives, you really can!

When it comes to replacing other forms of dairy, I like using oat milk as a 1:1 replacement for any type of milk in a recipe—and have been using it successfully for a long time. I recently started substituting cultured oat butter for dairy butter, and I recommend it as well. For a sour cream or crema replacement, I like Kite Hill vegan sour cream or the Vegan Crema on page 37, respectively.

Pico de Gallo

Habanana Sauce

Honey Chipotle Sauce

Green Tomatillo Salsa

Corn Salsa

Mango Salsa

Salsas Galore!

Chimichurri

Cantaloupe Cucumber Sauce

Peach Habanero Salsa

Roasted Tomato Salsa

PICO DE GALLO

**MAKES 2½ CUPS
(ENOUGH FOR 2 BATCHES
OF NACHOS)**

Takes about 15 minutes

2 vine-ripened tomatoes, diced
(1½ cups)

½ small yellow onion, peeled
and diced (½ cup)

2 jalapeños, stemmed, seeded,
and diced (½ cup)

10 sprigs fresh cilantro,
chopped (¼ cup)

1 clove garlic, peeled and
grated, plus extra as needed

2 tablespoons fresh lime juice
(from 1 to 2 limes), plus extra
as needed

¼ teaspoon kosher salt, plus
extra as needed

Pico is easily the recipe I have made most in my life in terms of volume and frequency. At the burrito shop, we used to make it in a 20-quart batch that would last only two days. At home, I whip it up anytime I have people over, or make tacos, or just feel like having something to snack on over a long weekend.

One of my favorite things about pico de gallo is the name, which translates to "rooster's beak." Some say the name was given because pico was traditionally eaten with your fingers, emulating a rooster picking at its food. Another theory is that pico looks like bird feed, and some say the name originated because one of the ingredients sometimes used, the serrano pepper, is shaped like a beak. In any case, it's a fun bit of trivia to break out next time you make it!

Stir all of the ingredients together in a large bowl to combine. Adjust the garlic, lime juice, and salt to taste. The pico de gallo will keep in an airtight container in the fridge for up to 5 days.

THE PICO RATIO

The ratios in this recipe are a great guideline for making any chunky salsa. Start with the main fruit or veggie—in this case, it's tomatoes—and add a little onion, a hot pepper or something spicy, an herb, garlic, citrus, and salt! For more ideas on how to play within this format, see Make Your Own Fresh Salsa! on page 19.

MANGO SALSA

Fruit salsas have gained a lot of popularity recently. I think they taste best when the fruit is the star, as in this mango version where the mango replaces the tomato in a classic pico ratio (see Box, page 14).

Stir all of the ingredients together in a large bowl to combine. Adjust the garlic, lime juice, and salt to taste. The salsa will keep in an airtight container in the fridge for up to 5 days.

**MAKES 2½ CUPS
(ENOUGH FOR 2 BATCHES
OF NACHOS)**
Takes about 15 minutes

1 large ripe mango, peeled,
  pitted, and diced (1½ cups)

½ small red onion, peeled and
  diced (½ cup)

2 Fresnos, stemmed, seeded,
  and diced (½ cup)

10 sprigs fresh cilantro
  (stems removed from half),
  chopped (¼ cup)

1 clove garlic, peeled and
  grated, plus extra as needed

2 tablespoons fresh lime juice
  (from 1 to 2 limes), plus extra
  as needed

¼ teaspoon kosher salt, plus
  extra as needed

PEACH HABANERO SALSA

**MAKES 2 CUPS
(ENOUGH FOR 2 BATCHES
OF NACHOS)**

Takes about 15 minutes

2 peaches, peeled, pitted, and
diced (about 1½ cups)

2 habaneros, stemmed,
seeded, and minced

1 clove garlic, peeled and
grated

2 tablespoons minced red
onion

2 tablespoons chopped fresh
cilantro

¼ teaspoon kosher salt, plus
extra as needed

I used to say that the cantaloupe salsa on page 17 was my favorite but . . . can I have two favorites? My wife, Georgina, will tell you that I call lots of things my favorite. I just like a lot of things, okay!? Speaking of Georgina, we gave away peach habanero hot sauce as our wedding favor—it was pretty much just this salsa blended up with extra vinegar. I always suggest making this with fresh in-season peaches, but I have done it with frozen, too, and it works (cut the peaches while they're still slightly frozen, but wait until they're fully thawed before serving).

Stir all of the ingredients together in a large bowl to combine. Adjust the salt to taste. The salsa will keep in an airtight container in the fridge for up to 5 days.

Variation

WEDDING FAVOR PEACH HABANERO HOT SAUCE:
Add ¼ cup of red wine vinegar to the salsa and pulse in a blender until smooth. The hot sauce will keep in an airtight container in the fridge for up to 1 month.

CANTALOUPE CUCUMBER SALSA

The mint and cucumber in this salsa make it very refreshing, and the cantaloupe adds a nice sweetness. It is a perfect counterpoint to salty, meaty, or spicy nachos. I especially love it with the Beef Bulgogi Nachos (page 120) or Mushroom Tofu Nachos (page 131).

Stir all of the ingredients together in a large bowl to combine. Adjust the garlic, lime juice, honey, and salt to taste. The salsa will keep in an airtight container in the fridge for up to 5 days.

MAKES 2½ CUPS
(ENOUGH FOR 2 BATCHES
OF NACHOS)
Takes about 15 minutes

½ English cucumber, diced
(¾ cup)

¼ cantaloupe, rind removed
and diced (¾ cup)

½ small red onion, peeled and
diced (½ cup)

½ red bell pepper, stemmed,
seeded, and diced (½ cup)

About 20 fresh mint leaves,
chopped (¼ cup)

1 clove garlic, peeled and
grated, plus extra as needed

2 tablespoons fresh lime juice
(from 1 to 2 limes), plus extra
as needed

1 teaspoon honey, plus extra as
needed

¼ teaspoon kosher salt , plus
extra as needed

CORN SALSA

**MAKES 2½ CUPS
(ENOUGH FOR 2 BATCHES
OF NACHOS)**
Takes about 15 minutes

1½ cups corn kernels, fresh
(from about 3 ears) or frozen

¼ teaspoon kosher salt, plus
more as needed

½ cup diced red bell pepper
(about ½ pepper)

3 scallions, trimmed and green
and white parts thinly sliced

10 sprigs fresh cilantro
(stems removed from half),
chopped (¼ cup)

1 clove garlic, peeled and
grated

Juice of 1 lime

1 tablespoon red wine vinegar

This style of corn salsa is meant to work in concert with other things; it's not really something you would serve on its own with chips. It's inspired by the corn salsa you find at some burrito places rather than the kind you might get in a jar at the grocery store, meaning it is a little less saucy and more focused on the corn itself. If you wanted to do a more well-rounded salsa with corn in it, one you could dip a chip into, I would suggest adding a little corn to either the Roasted Tomato Salsa on page 22 or the Pico de Gallo on page 14.

1 Preheat the broiler to high with a rack about 4 inches from the heat.

2 Spread the corn out on a sheet pan. Season with the ¼ teaspoon salt. Broil the corn until it begins to brown in places, about 5 minutes. (Watch carefully to make sure it doesn't burn.) Remove from the heat and let cool.

3 Pour the corn into a large bowl. Add the bell pepper, scallions, cilantro, garlic, lime juice, and vinegar and stir to combine. Allow to sit for 30 minutes so the flavors meld, then add more salt to taste.

4 Serve immediately or store in an airtight container in the fridge for up to 5 days.

MAKE YOUR OWN FRESH SALSA!

Anything can be salsafied! If you look at the recipes on pages 14 to 18, you can see that making salsa can be as simple as following a basic formula:

1½ cups main ingredient: This should be a fresh fruit or veggie that tastes good raw on its own. You can do a blend!

½ cup chopped onion: Use red, yellow, white, or even scallions.

½ cup chopped pepper: Use jalapeño, Fresno, bell, poblano, or others. If you are using super-hot peppers like habanero, you might want to use a little less unless you really love the heat.

¼ cup chopped fresh herbs: Cilantro is the obvious choice, but I love using mint or parsley for a twist.

2 tablespoons freshly squeezed citrus juice: Lime is the most common in salsas, but lemon or orange works great too! Why not try grapefruit!?

1 clove garlic, peeled and grated, and ¼ teaspoon salt (or more to taste): Essentials in any good salsa!

Here's a mix-and-match table of salsa ingredients. I left a bunch of rows empty so you can fill in your own ideas.

MAIN INGREDIENT	ONION	PEPPER	FRESH HERB	CITRUS JUICE
Pineapple	Yellow	Jalapeño	Cilantro	Lime
Pear	White	Cherry	Chervil	Orange
Strawberries	Red	Jalapeño	Baby spinach	Lemon
Pomegranate seeds and grapefruit segments (I make this every year at Christmas!)	Red	Jalapeño	Mint	Grapefruit and lime

TWO HOT SAUCE-Y SALSAS

MAKES 2 CUPS (ENOUGH FOR SEVERAL BATCHES OF NACHOS)

Takes about 15 minutes

Both of these sauces are right on the borderline between hot sauce and salsa. They both round out a nice chip and dip spread, giving the hotheads a good option, and have sweet elements that make the fire bearable.

I have a special soft spot for the Habanana Sauce. It was an off-menu item that I created for the burrito shop where I worked. I often made it for personal use, but I told one too many customers about it, and eventually, word got out. Enough people started asking for it that it became an official secret sauce with a cult following. I eventually ended up making it when I competed on *Guy's Grocery Games*, and it had all the judges sweating.

Although it *is* really hot, using only half of the habanero seeds and adding the banana balances the heat and brings the temp down a bit. And of course it's a hot sauce, so you use it sparingly. You could also take out all the seeds for a milder version.

The other salsa, Honey Chipotle Sauce, is made from canned chipotles in adobo. The adobo sauce is already packed with flavor, but I like to add some shallot and garlic and a good amount of honey to balance out the smoky heat from the peppers. I also find that canned chipotles can range in heat (sometimes they're very spicy!), so often I scrape the seeds from the peppers as insurance. Make no mistake though—this sauce is meant to be hot!

HABANANA SAUCE

Combine all of the ingredients in a food processor and process until smooth but textured, pausing to scrape down the bowl as needed. Use immediately or pour into an airtight container and store in the fridge for up to 2 weeks.

NOTE: This may go without saying, but you'll want to be really careful when handling the habaneros (or any spicy pepper, for that matter). The oils can get on your fingers—and then into your eyes or anywhere else you happen to touch. Some people like to wear gloves when handling these. I don't (not because I'm trying to be tough, but because I really don't like gloves!), but I do wash my hands really well with soap and warm water after touching or cutting habaneros or other hot peppers.

2 ripe bananas (the peels should be yellow with spots of black), peeled

20 habaneros, stemmed, half of the seeds removed (see Note)

¼ small yellow onion, peeled and diced

10 sprigs fresh cilantro (with stems)

1 clove garlic, peeled and roughly chopped

Juice of 1 lime

2 tablespoons red wine vinegar

½ teaspoon kosher salt

HONEY CHIPOTLE SAUCE

Combine all of the ingredients in a food processor and process until smooth but textured, pausing to scrape down the bowl as needed. Use immediately or pour into an airtight container and store in the fridge for up to 2 weeks.

1 can (7 ounces) chiles in adobo

1 jalapeño, stemmed (seeds removed if you prefer milder heat) and roughly chopped

2 plum tomatoes, cored

1 shallot, peeled and roughly chopped

1 clove garlic, peeled and roughly chopped

¼ cup honey

¼ cup red wine vinegar

¼ teaspoon kosher salt

ROASTED RED AND GREEN SALSAS

MAKES 2 CUPS (ENOUGH FOR 2 BATCHES OF NACHOS)

Takes about 25 minutes

I love these red and green salsas for most chip dipping situations, but they also work in recipes like the Baked Tomatillo Chicken on page 57 or the Chilaquiles on page 134.

ROASTED TOMATO SALSA

6 plum tomatoes, cored and quartered

2 jalapeños, stemmed (seeds removed if you prefer milder heat)

½ medium yellow onion, peeled and quartered

¼ teaspoon plus 1 pinch kosher salt

1 tablespoon olive oil

1 clove garlic, peeled

¼ cup chopped fresh cilantro

¼ cup red wine vinegar

1 Preheat the oven to 450°F.

2 Combine the tomatoes, jalapeños, and onion on a sheet pan, sprinkle with the ¼ teaspoon of salt, and drizzle with the olive oil. Toss to coat and spread the vegetables out evenly on the pan. Roast undisturbed until lightly blackened around the edges, about 15 minutes. Remove from the heat and allow to cool to room temperature.

3 Transfer the vegetables, including any cooking liquids, from the sheet pan to the bowl of a food processor. Add the garlic, cilantro, and vinegar and an additional pinch of salt. Pulse in the food processor until mostly smooth with small chunks.

4 Use immediately or pour into an airtight container and store in the fridge for up to 5 days.

GREEN TOMATILLO SALSA

1 Preheat the oven to 450°F.

2 Combine the tomatillos, jalapeños, and onion on a sheet pan, sprinkle with the ¼ teaspoon of salt, and drizzle with the olive oil. Toss to coat and spread the vegetables out evenly on the pan. Roast undisturbed until lightly blackened around the edges, about 15 minutes. Remove from the heat and allow to cool to room temperature.

3 Transfer the vegetables, including any cooking liquids, from the sheet pan to the bowl of a food processor. Add the garlic, cilantro, and vinegar and an additional pinch of salt. Pulse in the food processor until mostly smooth with small chunks.

4 Use immediately or pour into an airtight container and store in the fridge for up to 5 days.

8 tomatillos, husks removed, rinsed, and quartered

2 jalapeños, stemmed (seeds removed if you prefer milder heat)

½ medium yellow onion, peeled and quartered

¼ teaspoon plus 1 pinch kosher salt

1 tablespoon olive oil

1 clove garlic, peeled

¼ cup chopped fresh cilantro

¼ cup red wine vinegar

CHIMICHURRI

**MAKES ABOUT ¾ CUP
(ENOUGH FOR 1 BATCH
OF NACHOS)**
Takes about 5 minutes

2 cups fresh flat-leaf parsley

½ cup fresh oregano

1 clove garlic, peeled

½ cup olive oil, plus extra for
storage

2 tablespoons red wine vinegar

¼ teaspoon kosher salt

**NACHO
INSPO!**

▶ Carne Asada (page 55),
corn, Nacho Cheese Sauce
(page 7), and Chimichurri

▶ Cilantro Lime Shrimp
(page 61), shredded
cheddar cheese, Pico
de Gallo (page 14), and
Chimichurri

▶ Cumin-Roasted
Cauliflower (page 47),
shredded Gruyère cheese,
Chimichurri, and Power
Crema (page 36)

Chimichurri is an Argentinian sauce traditionally served with grilled meats. The baseline version includes chopped fresh parsley, garlic, and olive oil, but it is common to add other herbs and seasonings like oregano or red wine vinegar. It's easy to make, customizable to your personal tastes, and packed with flavor. It is one of those sauces that makes anything taste amazing, nachos included. I like switching up the herbs depending on my mood and the season, and I sometimes make it in a food processor or with a knife to play with the texture. I've given you both options here.

1 Place the parsley, oregano, garlic, olive oil, vinegar, and salt in the bowl of a food processor and process until combined and there are no more large leaves or stems. (Alternatively, finely chop the herbs on a cutting board. Add the salt and garlic right on the cutting board and continue to chop until the garlic and herbs are minced. Transfer to a bowl and stir in the oil and vinegar until combined.)

2 Transfer to an airtight container and top with an additional drizzle of olive oil, which will help prevent the herbs from browning. Use immediately or cover and store in the fridge for up to 4 days.

Variations

OTHER HERBS YOU CAN ADD TO CHIMICHURRI:

Use sparingly:
Rosemary
Sage
Thyme

Use aggressively:
Basil
Cilantro

JICAMA SLAW

I am not sure if I actually love this slaw or really just love Tajín seasoning, but, *man*, do I love Tajín, which is a chile-lime seasoning. This slaw is so fresh and delicious, it will brighten up any dish while also adding a little kick. Jicama is somewhat similar to a radish or water chestnut with its crunchy, refreshing texture and slight sweetness, and it goes great with the tart and spicy Tajín seasoning.

Combine the jicama, Tajín, cilantro, lime juice, and salt in a large bowl and toss together to coat. Taste and add more Tajín if you want. (I usually do.) Serve immediately or store in an airtight container in the fridge for up to 3 days.

NOTE: To prepare jicama, use a chef's knife to cut off the root end. Steady the jicama on a flat surface, then use shallow downward strokes to cut away the papery skin or any dry surface areas to reveal the flesh inside. Use a knife or julienne peeler to cut the inside into thin julienne slices for this slaw.

MAKES 2 CUPS (ENOUGH FOR 1 BATCH OF NACHOS)
Takes about 10 minutes

1 jicama, peeled and julienne sliced (see Note)

1 tablespoon Tajín seasoning, plus more as needed

2 tablespoons chopped fresh cilantro

Juice of 1 lime

Pinch of kosher salt

NACHO INSPO!

▶ Use on BBQ Pulled Pork Nachos (page 117) instead of regular slaw.

▶ Top any seafood nacho (see pages 92 and 94) with it.

▶ It's also great in a burrito!

TWO CABBAGE SLAWS

MAKES 4 CUPS (ENOUGH FOR 2 BATCHES OF NACHOS)

Takes about 10 minutes, plus 30 minutes of rest

Cold, crunchy slaw is a great addition to any taco, but you might be surprised to know that it works equally well on nachos. You need to chop it a little extra so it sits conveniently on individual chips instead of draping over multiple chips. I sway back and forth between using mayo or not for slaw, so in case you're like me, I've given you one of each.

CREAMY CRUNCHY SLAW

1 cup shredded red cabbage
(about ¼ cabbage)

2 cups shredded green
cabbage (about ½ cabbage)

1 cup shredded carrot
(about 1 large carrot)

1 teaspoon kosher salt

Juice of 1 lime

¼ cup mayo

2 tablespoons sour cream

Dash of hot sauce

1 Rinse the red cabbage in a strainer under running water and drain well. (This prevents the red cabbage from dyeing the entire mixture purple.) Roughly chop both the cabbages (you want to eliminate any very long strands that would hang awkwardly off the chips).

2 Place the cabbage in a large bowl, add the carrot, salt, lime juice, mayo, sour cream, and hot sauce, and toss to combine.

3 Allow to rest in the fridge for 30 minutes before serving. The slaw will keep in an airtight container in the fridge for up to 3 days.

BRIGHT VINEGARY SLAW

1 Rinse the red cabbage in a strainer under running water and drain well. (This prevents the red cabbage from dyeing the entire mixture purple.) Roughly chop both the cabbages (you want to eliminate any very long strands that would hang awkwardly off the chips).

2 Place the cabbage in a large bowl, add the carrot, salt, lime juice, cilantro, and vinegar, and toss to combine.

3 Allow to rest in the fridge for 30 minutes before serving. The slaw will keep in an airtight container in the fridge for up to 3 days.

1 cup shredded red cabbage (about ¼ cabbage)

2 cups shredded green cabbage (about ½ cabbage)

1 cup shredded carrot (about 1 large carrot)

1 teaspoon kosher salt

Juice of 1 lime

¼ cup chopped fresh cilantro

¼ cup red wine vinegar

QUICK PICKLED VEGGIES

MAKES 2 CUPS (ENOUGH FOR 1 BATCH OF NACHOS)
Takes about 15 minutes, plus 1 hour of rest

The bright kick from pickled veggies on top of nachos is a key element of the dish. You can quick-pickle carrots, radishes, and almost any other veggie with the same exact process, but red onion is my favorite. Bell peppers, chiles, or cauliflower, however, require a slightly different process that we will cover on the next page.

PICKLED CARROT, ONION, AND/OR RADISH

2 cups thinly sliced carrot, red onion, radish, or a mixture

1 cup red wine vinegar

1 teaspoon kosher salt

1 clove garlic, peeled

1 tablespoon sugar

1 Place the veggies in a 16-ounce mason jar or other tall airtight container. (If using a combination of vegetables, toss them together in a medium-size bowl before packing them into the jar.)

2 Combine the vinegar with 1 cup water in a medium-size bowl. Stir in the salt, garlic, and sugar and microwave for 1 minute. Stir the mixture until the sugar dissolves (microwave it in additional 15-second increments, stirring between each, if needed). You could heat up this brine on the stove top in a saucepan over medium heat if you do not have a microwave. Allow it to cool for 10 minutes.

3 Pour the brine over the veggies in the jar. Cover with the lid and refrigerate for at least 1 hour but preferably overnight. The pickles will keep in the fridge for up to 2 weeks (their flavors will intensify the longer they sit).

PICKLED PEPPERS AND/OR CAULIFLOWER

1 Place the veggies in a 16-ounce mason jar or other tall airtight container. (If using a combination of vegetables, toss them together in a medium-size bowl before packing them into the jar.)

2 Combine the vinegar with 1 cup water in a medium-size bowl. Stir in the salt, garlic, sugar, mustard seeds, and oregano and microwave for about 1 minute. Stir the mixture until the sugar dissolves (microwave it in additional 15-second increments, stirring between each, if needed). You could heat up this brine on the stove top in a saucepan over medium heat if you do not have a microwave. Allow it to cool for 10 minutes.

3 Pour the brine over the veggies in the jar. Cover with the lid and refrigerate for at least 1 hour but preferably overnight. The pickles will keep in the fridge for up to 2 weeks (their flavors will intensify the longer they sit).

NOTE: For peppers, feel free to use bell peppers or chiles (I like jalapeños) or a combination.

2 cups sliced peppers and/or bite-size cauliflower florets (see Note)

1 cup distilled white vinegar

1 teaspoon kosher salt

1 clove garlic, peeled

2 tablespoons sugar

1 teaspoon mustard seeds

½ teaspoon dried oregano flakes

GUACAMOLE

Here's the most important element of amazing guac: the perfect avocado. To improve your chances of achieving that, be selective at the store. I always use Hass avocados, and I find that ones with smooth thin skin are better than the thicker bumpier kind. Bigger avocados are generally better as well. They should be tender to the touch, but another way to tell when they are ripe is the stem will fall off. When you open the avocado, it will be dry and not juicy. But also know that if your avocado disappoints, you can still make something mighty tasty from it.

For me personally, the only things guac *truly* needs after a great avocado are salt and lime. Most of the time, I also add garlic and, less frequently, cilantro. Sometimes I toss in onion and tomato (usually when the avocados aren't the best), or I just add a spoonful of fresh Pico de Gallo (page 14) or Chimichurri (page 24), which does the trick.

MAKES ABOUT 2 CUPS (ENOUGH FOR 1 BATCH OF NACHOS)
Takes about 15 minutes

2 ripe avocados

½ teaspoon kosher salt

Juice of 1 lime, plus extra for storing

1 clove garlic, peeled and grated

2 tablespoons chopped fresh cilantro

1 tablespoon minced white onion (optional)

1 tablespoon minced jalapeño (optional)

2 tablespoons diced tomato (optional)

1 Halve and pit the avocados and scoop the flesh into a medium-size bowl. Add the salt and lime juice and mix well to coat, mashing gently with a fork or potato masher.

2 Add the garlic and cilantro, then the onion, jalapeño, and tomato (if using), and continue to mix and mash until combined. Serve immediately.

NOTE: Guac is best eaten shortly after it's made, but if you want to store it, spoon it into an airtight container. Tap the container on the counter to remove as many air bubbles as possible. Squeeze some additional lime juice over the top to prevent browning, cover with a piece of plastic wrap directly touching the surface of the guac, then cover with the lid. The guac will keep in the fridge for up to 2 days. If any browning occurs, scrape off the brown parts and stir the guac before serving.

GUA-PTIONS

MAKES ABOUT 2 CUPS (ENOUGH FOR 1 BATCH OF NACHOS)

Takes about 15 minutes

t's okay to be a purist about your guacamole, but sometimes it can be fun and delicious to switch things up. Here are two varieties that are in my regular rotation ; check out the gua-ptions opposite for more ideas.

BLT GUAC

2 ripe avocados

½ teaspoon kosher salt

Juice of 1 lemon

2 tablespoons mayo

1 clove garlic, peeled and grated

¼ cup chopped arugula, plus extra for garnish

¼ cup diced tomato, plus extra for garnish

¼ cup crumbled cooked bacon, plus extra for garnish

1 Halve and pit the avocados and scoop the flesh into a medium-size bowl. Add the salt, lemon juice, and mayo and mix well to coat, mashing gently with a fork or potato masher.

2 Add the garlic, arugula, tomato, and bacon and continue to mix and mash until combined. Garnish with additional arugula, tomato, and bacon and serve.

POMEGRANATE-MINT GUAC

1 Halve and pit the avocados and scoop the flesh into a medium-size bowl. Add the salt and orange juice and mix well to coat, mashing gently with a fork or potato masher.

2 Add the garlic, mint, and pomegranate seeds and continue to mix and mash until combined. Garnish with additional mint and pomegranate seeds and serve.

2 ripe avocados

½ teaspoon kosher salt

2 tablespoons fresh orange juice

1 clove garlic, peeled and grated

2 tablespoons chopped fresh mint, plus extra for garnish

¼ cup pomegranate seeds, plus extra for garnish

MORE GUA-PTIONS!

GUACAMOLE STYLE	Veggies	Herbs and Spices	Citrus Juice	Wildcard 1	Wildcard 2
BANH MI AS GUAC	Grated garlic and ginger, minced cucumber	Mint and cilantro	Lime	Fish sauce	Pickled carrot and radish (store-bought or homemade; see page 28)
PIZZA GUAC	Grated garlic	Dried oregano and crushed red pepper flakes	Lemon	Diced pepperoni	Grated Parmesan
GUAC-HUMM-OLE	Grated garlic	Parsley	Lemon	Hummus (a few spoonfuls)	Crunchy chickpeas and a drizzle of olive oil
BUFFALO CHICKEN	Diced carrot and celery	Parsley	Lemon	Diced cooked chicken Frank's RedHot sauce	Blue cheese
EVERYTHING BAGEL	Minced cucumber	Scallions or chives	Lemon	Everything seasoning	Cream cheese
WATERMELON	Diced watermelon	Mint	Lime	Feta cheese	Jalapeño

GUASACACA

**MAKES 2 CUPS
(ENOUGH FOR 2 BATCHES
OF NACHOS)**

Takes about 15 minutes

2 ripe avocados

¼ cup red wine vinegar

Juice of 2 limes

2 tablespoons chopped yellow
onion

1 jalapeño, stemmed (seeds
removed if you prefer milder
heat) and chopped (¼ cup)

1 clove garlic, peeled

2 tablespoons chopped fresh
cilantro

2 tablespoons olive oil

Guasacaca is an avocado-based sauce from Venezuela that is traditionally drizzled on grilled meats after they come off the heat. It's sort of like a smooth guacamole on steroids—thanks to generous amounts of citrus juice and vinegar. (Bonus: The extra acids prevent the avocado from browning, making this a good sauce to mix up ahead of time and keep in the fridge.) It's super tasty on pretty much anything—especially nachos.

1 Halve and pit the avocados and scoop the flesh into a food processor or blender. Add the vinegar, lime juice, onion, jalapeño, garlic, cilantro, and olive oil and blend on high until smooth.

2 Use a funnel to pour into a squeeze bottle (or an airtight container) and store in the fridge for up to 5 days.

CREMA 5 WAYS

MAKES 1 TO 1½ CUPS (ENOUGH FOR 1 BATCH OF NACHOS)
Takes 10 to 15 minutes

That big glob of sour cream can be a fun addition to a nacho plate from time to time, but I have become obsessed with using crema instead. It's similar to sour cream but thinner, allowing you to spread the creamy flavor evenly over all the nachos. When I first made my own crema, I essentially just watered down sour cream with some milk, but then I started mixing things up with different liquids and adding new flavors, creating the variations you find here. Any of these can be made with regular dairy sour cream or vegan sour cream (I like the one made by Kite Hill). So grab a package of squeeze bottles—they're available online or at most cooking stores and usually sold in packs of two or six—and come along for the ride!

LIME CREMA

Slightly tangier and flowier than regular sour cream.

1 cup sour cream
Juice of 1 lime
Pinch of kosher salt

Place all the ingredients in a large bowl and stir to combine. Use a funnel to pour the mixture into a squeeze bottle. The crema will keep in the fridge for up to 4 days.

AVOCADO CREMA

1 cup sour cream

1 ripe avocado, pitted and peeled

Juice of 2 limes

Pinch of kosher salt

Amps up the creaminess of an avocado and is a great way to serve more people if you only have one avocado.

Place all the ingredients in a blender (or in a large bowl if you're using a hand blender) and pulse until smooth and creamy. Use a funnel to pour the mixture into a squeeze bottle. The crema will keep in the fridge for up to 4 days (it will start to brown over time as the avocado oxidizes).

POWER CREMA

1 cup sour cream

¼ cup mayo

Juice of 1 lime

Juice of 1 lemon

Pinch of kosher salt

This is my favorite crema version—the mayo adds depth and you don't need to break out the blender. You could add a pinch of garlic powder if you want.

Place all the ingredients in a large bowl and stir to combine. Use a funnel to pour the mixture into a squeeze bottle. The crema will keep in the fridge for up to 4 days.

HERBY CREMA

This is almost like a lighter, simpler version of tzatziki or raita.

Place all the ingredients in a blender (or in a large bowl if you're using a hand blender) and pulse until smooth and creamy. Use a funnel to pour the mixture into a squeeze bottle. The crema will keep in the fridge for up to 4 days.

¾ cup sour cream

½ cup Greek yogurt

Juice of 1 lemon

1 clove garlic, peeled and grated

Pinch of kosher salt

1 tablespoon chopped fresh flat-leaf parsley

1 tablespoon chopped fresh chives

VEGAN CREMA

This is my favorite way to replicate crema without using dairy.

Place all the ingredients in a blender (or in a large bowl if you're using a hand blender) and pulse until smooth and creamy. Use a funnel to pour the mixture into a squeeze bottle. The crema will keep in the fridge for up to 4 days (it will start to brown over time as the avocado oxidizes).

1 can (14 ounces) coconut milk

½ ripe avocado, pitted and peeled

Juice of 2 limes

Pinch of kosher salt

BASIC BLACK BEANS

**MAKES 2½ CUPS
(ENOUGH FOR 1 BATCH
OF NACHOS)**

*Takes about 5 hours
(mostly passive time)*

2 tablespoons olive oil

1 large yellow onion, peeled
and diced

1 jalapeño, stemmed, seeded,
and diced

3 cloves garlic, peeled and
minced

1 pound dried black beans,
soaked overnight and
drained

3 cups water or veggie stock

1 teaspoon kosher salt

1 teaspoon ground cumin

½ teaspoon dried oregano
flakes

½ tablespoon red wine vinegar

½ tablespoon sugar

It's always good to have a solid bean recipe in your back pocket. I like this one because it's vegan, versatile, and a great value. You can easily make this with canned beans if you want to get dinner on the table quickly. Or make this recipe in a slow cooker so you'll have perfect beans waiting for you when you get home from work.

1 Heat the olive oil in a large frying pan over medium-high heat. Add the onion and jalapeño and cook, stirring occasionally, until softened, about 5 minutes.

2 Add the garlic, stir to incorporate, and cook until the garlic is fragrant, about 1 minute.

3 Add the beans, water, salt, cumin, oregano, vinegar, and sugar. Stir well to combine. Reduce the heat to low and cover.

4 Cook, stirring once every hour or so, until the beans are tender, about 5 hours. The liquid should just barely cover the beans throughout cooking; add more liquid as needed if they start to dry out.

5 Serve hot or let cool and store in an airtight container in the fridge for up to 5 days.

Variations

TO MAKE WITH CANNED BLACK BEANS: Replace the dried beans with 1 can (28 ounces) black beans, strained and rinsed. Replace the 3 cups of water or stock with ½ cup. In Step 4, cook for 15 minutes instead of 5 hours.

TO MAKE WITH DRIED BEANS IN A SLOW COOKER: Complete Steps 1 and 2 in a frying pan. Add the sautéed mixture to a slow cooker and proceed from Step 3, cooking on low heat, covered, for 8 hours.

MEATY PINTO BEANS

Oftentimes restaurant pinto beans include a bit of meat, which may be hard to discern in terms of flavor or texture but also means they're not vegetarian. I say, if you are going to add meat to your beans, you might as well *add meat*! That's what I do here—and these meaty beans eat almost like a chili.

I like to grab the cheapest cut of bone-in fresh pork that's available at the grocery store. My favorite is when they have a package of three or four baby back ribs—I'll add those straight to the pot. By the time the beans are tender, I can fish the bones right out of the mix and the meat will be shredded throughout just from stirring the beans while they cook. If you have a slow cooker, you can prepare this as directed with the cooker set to low.

1 Preheat the oven to 325°F.

2 Add the beans to a large Dutch oven. Add the ribs, stock, onion, and garlic. Add the chipotles in adobo (sauce and all), vinegar, honey, mustard, cumin, oregano, and salt and stir well to combine.

3 Cover the pot and put it into the oven. Cook, stirring every couple of hours and making sure the beans don't dry out, until the beans are tender, 6 to 8 hours. (If the beans start to look dry, stir in a little water until they have the consistency of a chili.)

4 Serve hot or let cool and store in an airtight container in the fridge for up to 5 days.

NOTE: These beans are spicy. If you want milder beans, you can use half as many chipotle chiles and/or scrape the seeds out of the chipotles with a paring knife before adding them.

MAKES ABOUT 4 CUPS (ENOUGH FOR 2 TO 3 BATCHES OF NACHOS)
Takes 6 to 8 hours, plus overnight soaking

2 cups dried pinto beans, soaked overnight and drained

¾ pound baby back ribs (about 4 ribs), any silver skin removed

1 quart chicken or veggie stock

1 small yellow onion, peeled and diced

2 cloves garlic, peeled and minced

1 can (7 ounces) chipotle chiles in adobo (see Note)

½ cup apple cider vinegar

¼ cup honey

2 tablespoons yellow mustard

1 teaspoon ground cumin

1 teaspoon dried oregano flakes

2 teaspoons kosher salt

REFRIED BEANS

**MAKES ABOUT 1½ CUPS
(ENOUGH FOR 1 BATCH
OF NACHOS)**

Takes about 15 minutes

2 tablespoons bacon fat or
olive oil

¼ cup diced yellow onion, plus
extra for serving (optional)

1 tablespoon minced garlic

1½ cups cooked pinto beans
(store-bought or homemade;
see page 39)

1 cup chicken stock

Crumbled Cotija cheese,
for serving (optional)

Chopped fresh cilantro,
for serving (optional)

I grew up thinking refried beans were "just okay" because the ones I had always came from a can. Don't get me wrong, canned refrieds *are* good, but they don't come close to the ones made from scratch—even if you make them from canned beans! Truly homemade refrieds come out so creamy and delicious and are amazing on nachos. When using them on nachos, make sure to add a little extra liquid so they have an almost saucy consistency (which is best for even distribution on the chips).

1 Heat the bacon fat in a medium-size saucepan over medium heat.

2 Add the onion and cook, stirring occasionally, until softened, about 10 minutes. Add the garlic and cook, stirring, until fragrant, about 1 minute.

3 Add the beans and chicken stock and stir to combine. Bring to a simmer, cover, and reduce the heat to low. Cook until some of the liquid has evaporated, about 10 minutes.

4 Remove from the heat and mash the beans with a potato masher until they are just slightly chunky and everything is well combined.

5 Use hot atop nachos or garnish with diced onion, cheese, onion, and cilantro (if using) and serve. The refried beans can be stored in an airtight container in the fridge for up to 5 days. Before using them on nachos, warm them in a saucepan over low heat or in the microwave, adding just a little water to loosen them up.

RED CURRY CHICKPEAS

I first had red curry chickpeas in a burrito at a western Massachusetts burrito chain called Bueno Y Sano. I love that they embraced chickpeas as a nontraditional burrito ingredient by giving them a nontraditional flavor. You can make red curry paste from scratch if you want, but store-bought works great for these. Make sure to cook the chickpeas in the sauce so they get nice and soft and absorb the red curry flavor.

1 Heat the oil in a medium-size frying pan over medium heat. Add the curry paste and cook, stirring, until fragrant, about 5 minutes.

2 Add the chickpeas to the curry paste and stir to coat. Add the coconut milk and stir to combine.

3 Bring the chickpeas to a simmer, then reduce the heat to low. Simmer until the sauce thickens and coats the chickpeas and the chickpeas are very tender and creamy, about 30 minutes.

4 Serve hot or let cool and store in an airtight container in the fridge for up to 4 days.

MAKES 1 CUP (ENOUGH FOR 1 BATCH OF NACHOS)
Takes about 40 minutes

1 tablespoon vegetable oil

1 heaping tablespoon red curry paste

1 can (14 ounces) chickpeas, strained and rinsed

⅓ cup canned coconut milk (preferably full-fat but any will work)

NACHO INSPO!

▶ Red Curry Chickpeas and Vegan "Cheese" Sauce (page 10), topped with Chimichurri (page 24), Honey Chipotle Sauce (page 21), Vegan Crema (page 37), and lots of fresh cilantro

▶ Red Curry Chickpeas, Mexican-Style Chorizo (page 54), and Jack cheese, topped with Pico de Gallo (page 14) and Power Crema (page 36)

FAJITA-STYLE VEGGIES

**MAKES 2 CUPS
(ENOUGH FOR 1 BATCH
OF NACHOS)**

Takes about 15 minutes

1 tablespoon vegetable oil

1 large yellow onion, peeled
and cut into ½-inch-wide
slices

2 bell peppers (any color),
stemmed, seeded, and sliced
into ½-inch-wide strips

Kosher salt

Charred peppers and onions are a staple for fajita night, so why not put them on your nachos, too? I stuck to a classic combo for this recipe, but depending on your mood and the season, you can definitely add or swap in other veggies. For relatively quick-cooking vegetables like asparagus, broccoli florets, or chopped brussels sprouts, you can cook them as directed; if you want to add butternut squash or another root veggie, you will need to parcook it beforehand (see Note).

1 Heat the oil in a large heavy-bottomed frying pan over high heat.

2 Add the veggies and cook, stirring occasionally, until they are charred at the edges but retain some crunch in the center, 10 to 15 minutes. Season with kosher salt to taste.

3 Serve immediately or store in an airtight container in the fridge for up to 2 days.

NOTE: To parcook squash or potato for fajitas: Peel and cut the vegetable into 1-inch cubes. Toss with olive oil and salt and spread out on a sheet pan. Roast at 400°F until just about fork-tender but slightly undercooked, about 20 minutes. You can do this ahead of time and set them aside until you're ready to make the fajitas. Finish cooking them as directed in Step 2.

CRISPY ROASTED POTATOES

**MAKES 2 CUPS
(ENOUGH FOR 1 BATCH
OF NACHOS)**

Takes about 1 hour

1 pound small Yukon Gold
   or fingerling potatoes,
   scrubbed (unpeeled) and cut
   into 1-inch to 1½-inch pieces

2 tablespoons vegetable oil

2 tablespoons cornstarch

1 teaspoon kosher salt

1 teaspoon freshly cracked
   black pepper

NACHO INSPO!

▶ Raclette Nachos: Top chips
with the potatoes and sliced
cornichons. Pour melted
raclette cheese on top
before serving.

▶ Patatas Bravas Nachos:
Top chips with the potatoes,
cheddar cheese, and
Manchego and bake. After
baking, dollop with spicy
tomato sauce and mayo.

▶ Breakfast Burrito Nachos:
Top chips with the potatoes,
crumbled Mexican-Style
Chorizo (page 54), and
cheddar cheese and bake.
After baking, top with salsa
and fried egg(s).

Putting potatoes on nachos might seem weird at first, but consider a few facts: Potatoes with cheese are delicious. Potatoes in a breakfast burrito are delicious. Potatoes with crispy outsides and creamy tender middles are delicious. Need any more evidence? Soaking the potatoes in cold water before roasting helps remove excess starch and allows them to get extra crispy in the oven.

1 Put the potatoes in a large bowl and add cold water to cover them. Allow to soak for about 30 minutes. Drain the water from the bowl and pat the potatoes dry with a paper towel, using the same towel to remove excess water from the bowl.

2 Preheat the oven to 500°F with a rack in the top quarter of the oven (or 450°F if using the convection function).

3 Drizzle the oil over the potatoes in the bowl and toss to coat. Add the cornstarch, salt, and pepper and toss to coat.

4 Pour the potatoes onto a sheet pan and spread them out evenly.

5 Bake, flipping with a spatula about halfway through, until tender and browned evenly, about 20 minutes.

6 Use on nachos immediately or let cool and store in an airtight container in the fridge for up to 4 days. The sooner you use them, the crispier they will be. You can gently warm them in the oven or microwave before using on nachos.

BRAISED CABBAGE

Raw cabbage is often served with Mexican food in America, but its cooked cousin doesn't get as much love. This version is based on a traditional Mexican dish called tinga de repollo, which isn't as common in the States as it could be—and when you taste it, you might wonder why. The cabbage comes out tender and flavorful and finally ready for its moment to shine. The slight smoky kick from the chipotles is the perfect pairing for the earthy cabbage.

1 Heat the oil in a large frying pan over medium heat. Add the cabbage and stir to coat. Add the salt, pepper, and chipotle chiles and stir to combine. Cook, stirring occasionally, until the cabbage is slightly softened, about 2 minutes.

2 Stir in the vinegar and tomatoes. Bring to a simmer and reduce the heat to low. Cover and let simmer, stirring occasionally, until the cabbage is tender, about 30 minutes. (If the cabbage is too soupy in the last 5 minutes of cooking, uncover and allow some of the liquid to cook off.)

3 Serve hot or let cool and store in an airtight container in the fridge for up to 4 days.

MAKES ABOUT 2 CUPS (ENOUGH FOR 1 BATCH OF NACHOS)
Takes about 40 minutes

1 tablespoon olive oil
½ large head of green cabbage, cored and sliced ½ inch thick
2 teaspoons kosher salt
2 teaspoons freshly cracked black pepper
2 canned chipotle chiles in adobo, diced
1 tablespoon red wine vinegar
1 can (14 ounces) crushed tomatoes

NACHO INSPO!

▶ Cabbage Roll Nachos: Top chips with the cabbage, cooked ground beef, and Jack cheese. After baking, garnish with fresh parsley.

▶ Brats and Cabbage Nachos: Top chips with the cabbage, bratwurst slices, Swiss cheese, and caraway seeds. After baking, serve with a mustard crema (mix ¼ cup of Dijon mustard with the Power Crema on page 36).

CUMIN-ROASTED CAULIFLOWER

Charring cauliflower gives it such a nice toasty flavor that I sometimes can't believe it isn't always served this way. Crank your oven up high, and if it has a convection function, now is the time to use it! Bonus: This recipe can be prepared exactly the same way with quartered brussels sprouts.

MAKES ABOUT 4 CUPS (ENOUGH FOR 1 BATCH OF NACHOS)
Takes about 25 minutes

1 head of cauliflower, cored

2 tablespoons olive oil

1 tablespoon ground cumin

1 teaspoon smoked paprika

1 teaspoon garlic powder

1 teaspoon kosher salt

1 teaspoon freshly cracked black pepper

NACHO INSPO!

1 Preheat the oven to 500°F with a rack in the upper quarter of the oven (or 450°F if using the convection function).

2 Break up the cauliflower into bite-size florets, cutting some as needed to make them uniform in size. Transfer to a large bowl.

3 Drizzle the oil over the cauliflower and toss gently to coat. Add the cumin, paprika, garlic powder, salt, and pepper and toss well to coat.

4 Pour the cauliflower onto a sheet pan and spread it out evenly to make sure it's not crowded (otherwise it will steam instead of char).

5 Roast undisturbed until the cauliflower is tender and browned at the edges, about 15 minutes.

6 Serve hot or let cool and store in an airtight container in the fridge for up to 3 days.

▶ Use this cauliflower in place of chicken in any recipe—especially the Buffalo Chicken Nachos on page 84.

▶ Use it in nachos topped with Taleggio cheese and lots of caramelized onions.

JALAPEÑO MARGARITA GLAZED TOFU

MAKES 4 SERVINGS (ENOUGH FOR 1 BATCH OF NACHOS)

Takes about 25 minutes, plus 30 minutes of pressing

1 block (14 ounces) extra-firm tofu, drained and cut into 1-inch cubes

2 tablespoons vegetable oil

1 jalapeño, stemmed (seeds removed if you prefer milder heat) and diced

2 tablespoons of your favorite tequila

Juice of 1 lime

2 tablespoons agave nectar

NACHO INSPO!

▶ Bright and fresh: Jalapeño Margarita Glazed Tofu with Chihuahua cheese, topped with Jicama Slaw (page 25) and Cantaloupe Cucumber Salsa (page 17)

▶ Spicy and sweet: Jalapeño Margarita Glazed Tofu, Pepper Jack cheese and Fajita-Style Veggies (page 42), topped with Habanana Sauce (page 21), Mango Salsa (page 15), and Creamy Crunchy Slaw (page 26) to cool things down

My favorite margaritas and my favorite tofu recipes have something in common—both have a nice kick! This glazed tofu recipe takes inspiration from the best kind of margarita. Instead of honey, my usual margarita sweetener, I mixed in agave nectar to amplify the agave flavors in the tequila.

1 Line a plate with paper towels and spread the tofu evenly on top. Allow to dry until no longer wet to the touch, about 30 minutes.

2 Heat the oil in a large frying pan over high heat.

3 Add the tofu to the pan and cook until browned on the bottom, about 3 minutes. Toss the tofu in the pan, using a spatula to help turn it (it may want to stick, especially on the first side), and cook until browned, another 3 minutes.

4 Add the jalapeño and continue cooking, stirring often, until the jalapeño is soft and the tofu is browned all over, about 8 more minutes.

5 Remove from the heat and add the tequila, lime juice, and agave nectar to the pan, stirring gently to combine. The heat from the pan will cause the mixture to darken in color and thicken to a glaze. Stir for a minute or two as it thickens, then transfer the tofu and glaze to a bowl or serving plate.

6 Serve hot or let cool and store in an airtight container in the fridge for up to 4 days. Before using it on nachos, reheat it in a small saucepan over low heat or in the microwave.

TACO-STYLE GROUND BEEF

Taco meat was the first recipe I ever made, and it's still one of my favorite things to whip up. I always make it a little differently each time, but this is my base recipe. I call for beef here, but feel free to swap out half for ground turkey or chicken (or replace the beef entirely, in which case add more oil). This recipe even works well with vegan ground "meat"—if using a cooked variety (such as Gardein), begin the recipe on Step 3; if using a raw kind (such as Impossible Meat), just follow the recipe as is!

1 Heat the oil in a large frying pan over high heat.

2 Add the beef and season with the salt. Cook, stirring, until browned and cooked through, about 5 minutes. Remove the beef from the pan with a slotted spoon, leaving about 2 tablespoons of fat in the pan; set the beef aside.

3 Add the onion and jalapeños to the fat in the pan and cook, stirring occasionally, until the vegetables soften and start browning at the edges, about 10 minutes.

4 Stir in the garlic and cook until fragrant, about 1 minute. Return the beef to the pan and add the cumin, oregano, paprika, chili powder, coriander, and cloves. Cook, stirring, until the spices release their aroma, about 3 minutes.

5 Add the beer, vinegar, and honey and stir to incorporate. Bring the beef mixture to a simmer, then reduce the heat to low. Cook until the liquid has reduced and the beef is coated with a thick sauce, about 20 minutes.

6 Serve hot or let cool and store in an airtight container in the fridge for up to 4 days. Reheat it before using.

MAKES 1½ POUNDS (ENOUGH FOR 1 BATCH OF NACHOS)
Takes about 45 minutes

1 tablespoon vegetable oil

1½ pounds ground beef (90% lean)

1 teaspoon kosher salt

1 small yellow onion, peeled and diced

3 jalapeños, stemmed, seeded, and diced

3 cloves garlic, peeled and minced

1 tablespoon ground cumin

2 teaspoons dried oregano flakes

1 teaspoon smoked paprika

1 teaspoon chili powder

½ teaspoon ground coriander

Pinch of ground cloves

1 bottle (12 ounces) beer or hard cider, or 1½ cups stock or water

1 tablespoon red wine vinegar

1 tablespoon honey

CARNITAS

MAKES 2 POUNDS (ENOUGH FOR 2 TO 3 BATCHES OF NACHOS)

Takes about 3 hours (mostly passive time)

Juice of 2 limes

Juice of 1 orange

1 small yellow onion, peeled and quartered

5 cloves garlic, peeled

1 tablespoon ground cumin

2 tablespoons dried oregano flakes

½ teaspoon ground coriander

¼ teaspoon ground cloves

Pinch of ground cinnamon

1½ teaspoons kosher salt

2 pounds boneless, skinless pork shoulder, cut into 3-inch pieces (see Note)

Carnitas (the name means "little meats" in Spanish) is my 100%-always-order meat at any burrito place—I can't get enough of these flavorful, crispy-tender shreds of pork. Traditional carnitas is believed to have originated in the Michoacán region of Mexico, but the dish is popular throughout the country, and its preparation and ingredients vary based on the location and cook. This is my take on the dish, which I make in a baking dish in the oven and which is super tasty—but if you're interested in exploring true carnitas further, check out a recipe by Mexican chef Pati Jinich, which you can find in her books or online. You can also use a slow cooker to make this; follow the directions as written, setting the temperature to high.

1 Preheat the oven to 325°F.

2 Combine the lime juice, orange juice, onion, garlic, cumin, oregano, coriander, cloves, cinnamon, and 1 teaspoon of salt in a food processor or blender. Blend until smooth.

3 Put the pork in a large baking dish and season all over with the remaining ½ teaspoon of salt. Pour the sauce from the food processor over the pork and turn to coat.

4 Bake, stirring every 45 minutes, about 2½ hours, until the meat is falling apart.

5 Remove the pork from the oven and let cool slightly. If there is lots of excess fat, use a spoon to skim some of it off. (You want there to be a bit of fat in the dish—a thin layer shimmering on top of the pork is about right.)

6 Mash the pork right in the baking dish with a potato masher until it is shredded into bite-size pieces.

7 Serve hot or let cool and store in an airtight container in the fridge for up to 5 days.

NOTE: If you can't find pork shoulder, you can make this with pork stewing meat, but it may end up a little dry. I can usually find boneless, skinless pork shoulder at my store, but it is sometimes packaged as pork shoulder steaks and I have to take out the bone and cut them into quarters. I prefer doing this all before cooking because it makes it much easier in the end to shred the pork with the potato masher.

Variation

SPICY HABANERO CARNITAS: I also do a spicy version of this recipe, adding 5 habaneros to the blender in Step 2. I usually take the seeds out of 4 of them to make it spicy but not unbearable.

CONEY ISLAND–STYLE CHILI

You could put your favorite chili on nachos, but when I am looking for something to pour onto my chips, I personally don't like super-chunky homestyle chili. I prefer one like this— with a thinner Coney Island chili dog–style texture.

If you have your heart set on adding beans or corn or zucchini or any other favorite chili ingredient, go ahead and add it with the tomatoes. Just be aware that when simmering the chili, you might need to cover it for a portion of the time to control the liquid.

**MAKES ABOUT 4 CUPS
(ENOUGH FOR 2 BATCHES
OF NACHOS)**

Takes about 45 minutes

1 pound ground beef (85% lean)

1 small yellow onion, peeled
and diced

3 jalapeños, stemmed, seeded,
and diced

½ teaspoon kosher salt, plus
extra as needed

1 teaspoon freshly cracked
black pepper, plus extra as
needed

2 cloves garlic, peeled and
minced

1 tablespoon ground cumin

2 teaspoons smoked paprika

1 teaspoon chili powder

2 teaspoons dried oregano
flakes

½ teaspoon ground coriander

¼ teaspoon ground cinnamon

¼ teaspoon ground cloves

1 can (28 ounces) crushed
tomatoes

1 tablespoon apple cider vinegar

1 teaspoon sugar

Sour cream and fresh cilantro,
for garnish (optional)

1 Combine the beef, onion, and jalapeños in a large pot over
medium-high heat. Season with the salt and pepper and
cook, stirring, until the meat and veggies lightly brown,
about 15 minutes. Drain any excess fat if needed. The
mixture should be juicy and glistening with fat but not
swimming in it.

2 Add the garlic and cook, stirring often, until fragrant and
slightly golden, about 2 minutes.

3 Add the cumin, paprika, chili powder, oregano, coriander,
cinnamon, and cloves and cook until fragrant, about
1 minute.

4 Add the tomatoes, vinegar, and sugar and stir to combine.
Taste and add more salt and pepper if needed. Bring to a
simmer, then reduce the heat to low. Simmer, uncovered,
to thicken, about 20 minutes.

5 Serve hot, garnished with sour cream and cilantro, if desired,
or let cool and store in an airtight container in the fridge for
up to 5 days.

▶ Chili Dog Nachos: Layer tortilla chips with chili, chopped hot dogs,
and Nacho Cheese Sauce (page 7). After broiling, top with diced
raw onions and lots of sour cream.

▶ Loaded Potato Nachos: Layer tortilla chips with Crispy Roasted
Potatoes (page 44), crumbled cooked bacon, chili, and shredded
cheddar cheese. After broiling, top with lots of sour cream and
minced chives.

MEXICAN-STYLE CHORIZO

**MAKES 1½ POUNDS
(ENOUGH FOR 2 BATCHES
OF NACHOS)**
*Takes about 45 minutes,
plus an overnight rest*

½ pound pork belly

1½ pounds ground pork

1 small yellow onion, peeled
and quartered

7 cloves garlic, peeled

1 habanero, stemmed
(seeds removed if you
prefer milder heat)

½ cup red wine vinegar

1 tablespoon kosher salt

1 tablespoon smoked paprika

1 tablespoon chipotle powder

1 tablespoon chili powder

1 teaspoon ground cumin

1 teaspoon ground coriander

Pinch of ground cloves

Vegetable oil, for cooking

There are two kinds of chorizo, with different ingredients and textures. Spanish chorizo is dried and cured, a sliceable sausage similar to pepperoni (but with distinctive flavorings). Mexican chorizo is typically sold raw, either in links or loose, and has to be cooked before it's eaten. This recipe is my take on Mexican-style chorizo. It's one that I tested for the burrito shop that I managed; I tweaked it over and over and over again until I got it just right. All that testing paid off because it became a huge hit. It's one of my favorites and works great on literally any nacho. It has just the right amount of heat, but it is intensely flavored, so use it sparingly, about ¾ cup on a tray of nachos.

1 Use a sharp knife to cut the pork belly into ½-inch strips striped with fat (technically called lardons) and place them in a large bowl. Add the ground pork and mix with your hands to combine.

2 Combine the onion, garlic, habanero, vinegar, salt, paprika, chipotle powder, chili powder, cumin, coriander, and cloves in the bowl of a food processor and process until very smooth. Pour the mixture over the meat in the bowl and stir to combine thoroughly. Cover and refrigerate overnight.

3 Heat a little vegetable oil in a large frying pan over medium-low heat, then add the pork mixture along with any liquid from the bowl. Cook slowly, stirring often, until the meat cooks through and the pork belly has softened and its fat has rendered, about 30 minutes. Use a slotted spoon to transfer the mixture to a serving container, leaving behind the excess fat, but not all of it.

4 Serve hot or let cool and store in an airtight container in the fridge for up to 4 days. Reheat as needed in a frying pan over low heat or in the microwave.

CARNE ASADA

arne asada, whose name means "grilled meat" in Spanish, is my favorite type of beef to make and eat at home. It's easy to do, it uses an affordable cut, and it comes out perfect every time. Skirt steak is a great cut for marinating because it has lots of nooks and crannies that really allow a flavorful sauce to penetrate. Almost any way you cook or season it, as long as you cut it thinly against the grain, it will be perfectly tender.

1 Put the steak in a medium-size bowl or large ziplock bag.

2 Whisk together the vinegar, oil, garlic, Worcestershire, honey, cumin, and salt in a small bowl. Pour this mixture over the steak.

3 Cover and allow to marinate for at least 1 hour on the counter or up to 24 hours in the fridge.

4 When ready to cook, heat a grill or large cast-iron skillet to high. Transfer the steak to the grill or skillet (leave behind the marinade) and cook until browned on the bottom, about 6 minutes. Turn the steak with tongs and cook until it is browned on the bottom and the internal temperature reaches 145°F, about 6 minutes, depending on the thickness of the steak.

5 Allow to cool for about 10 minutes before thinly slicing against the grain.

6 Serve warm or let cool and store in an airtight container in the fridge for up to 4 days.

MAKES ABOUT 1¼ POUNDS (ENOUGH FOR 1 BATCH OF NACHOS)
Takes 30 minutes, plus 1 hour for marinating

1½ pounds skirt steak

¼ cup red wine vinegar

2 tablespoons vegetable oil

1 clove garlic, peeled and grated

1 tablespoon Worcestershire sauce

1 tablespoon honey

1 teaspoon ground cumin

1 teaspoon kosher salt

BRAISED LAMB BEERBACOA

**MAKES 1½ POUNDS
(ENOUGH FOR 1 TO 2
BATCHES OF NACHOS)**

*Takes about 5 hours
(mostly passive time)*

2 tablespoons vegetable oil

2 pounds boneless lamb
shoulder, cut into 2-inch
cubes

2 medium yellow onions,
peeled and diced

1 jalapeño, stemmed, seeded,
and diced

5 cloves garlic, peeled and
minced

3 cups pale ale or beef or
chicken stock (or water)

4 canned chipotle chiles in
adobo, plus 2 tablespoons
adobo sauce from the can

1 tablespoon ground cumin

1 tablespoon dried oregano
flakes

¼ cup apple cider vinegar

2 tablespoons honey

This recipe is inspired by Mexican barbacoa, a dish of tasty shredded meat that is sometimes made with beef, but more often goat or lamb (and depending on the region, a variety of other animal proteins). Beef barbacoa is common in American fast-casual restaurants as a filling for burritos and tacos, but in Mexico barbacoa is more of a special-occasion dish and the protein, seasonings, and preparation vary depending on the geography and cook. You can use beef in this particular recipe if you wish, but I suggest you try it with lamb because it is richer and has deeper flavors and more umami. I like to add beer to this—not only because I can call it *beerbacoa* but because I like the flavor twist. Feel free to use water or stock for a more traditional (and gluten-free) version. If you want to make this even more hands-off, complete Step 3 in the oven at 275°F.

1 Heat the vegetable oil in a large heavy-bottomed pot over high heat. Add the lamb and sear, turning occasionally, until browned on all sides, about 2 minutes per side. Transfer the lamb to a plate and set aside.

2 Reduce the heat to medium-high. Add the onions and jalapeño and cook, stirring occasionally, until the veggies are softened and just starting to brown around the edges, about 10 minutes. Add the garlic and cook until fragrant and slightly golden, about 2 minutes.

3 Add the ale and return the meat to the pot. Make sure to stir and scrape the bottom of the pot to incorporate the browned bits into the sauce. Add the chipotles and adobo sauce, then the cumin, oregano, vinegar, and honey. Bring to a simmer. Cook, covered and stirring occasionally, for about 2 hours. Uncover and continue to cook until the liquid reduces and the meat is tender and pierces very easily with a fork, about 2 hours more.

4 Remove the pot from the heat and gently shred the lamb with a potato masher right in its own sauce.

5 Serve hot or let cool and store in an airtight container in the fridge for up to 4 days.

Variation: I also do a coffee-based version of this recipe, substituting for the ale with 1½ cups of brewed coffee, ½ cup of milk, and 1 cup of stock.

BAKED TOMATILLO CHICKEN

This recipe has the best ratio of difficulty to deliciousness. Pour some sauce on the chicken, throw it in the oven, wait a little bit, eat. I love making this recipe with store-bought tomatillo salsa and serving it over rice for the easiest meal ever.

The sauce is so delicious. I prefer to make it with coconut milk instead of dairy milk because I think it keeps the final dish lighter and the sauce is less likely to curdle, but I have seen similar versions prepared with regular milk or even heavy cream. The finished sauce is creamy and tart, and the poached chicken is juicy and tender.

MAKES 2 CHICKEN BREASTS (ENOUGH FOR 2 BATCHES OF NACHOS)
Takes about 1 hour

2 boneless, skinless chicken breasts

Kosher salt

1 cup green tomatillo salsa (store-bought or homemade; see page 23)

½ cup coconut milk or whole milk

1 Preheat the oven to 350°F.

2 Place the chicken breasts into a baking dish in which they fit snugly. Season with a pinch of salt.

3 Stir together the salsa and coconut milk in a small bowl and pour it over the chicken in the baking dish.

4 Bake until the chicken is cooked through, 45 minutes to 1 hour.

5 Allow to cool for 5 minutes before thinly slicing crosswise.

6 Serve hot with its cooking liquid or let cool and store in an airtight container in the fridge for up to 4 days.

CHILI-LIME GRILLED CHICKEN

**MAKES 1½ POUNDS
(ENOUGH FOR 2 BATCHES
OF NACHOS)**

*Takes about 20 minutes, plus at
least 30 minutes for marinating*

½ cup fresh lime juice
(from 4 to 6 limes)

2 tablespoons honey

½ tablespoon chili powder

1 teaspoon ground cumin

1 clove garlic, peeled and
grated

¼ cup chopped fresh cilantro
(from about 10 sprigs)

½ teaspoon kosher salt

2 tablespoons olive oil

1½ pounds boneless, skinless
chicken breasts, sliced in half
the flat way to make them
thinner

This chicken comes out tender, juicy, and flavorful and works anytime you need chicken for nachos, tacos, burritos, or just a backyard BBQ. Having such a citrus-forward marinade for chicken is a gift and a curse. It's great because it works fast—you can marinate it for as little as a half hour—but it can be tricky because if you leave the chicken in the marinade too long, the lime will start to change the texture of the chicken the same way it would "cook" fish in ceviche. Be careful not to overmarinate it.

1 Mix the lime juice, honey, chili powder, cumin, garlic, cilantro, and salt in a large bowl. Transfer 1/4 cup of this marinade mixture to a small bowl and set it aside in the fridge.

2 Stir the oil into the remaining marinade in the large bowl. Add the chicken and turn to coat. Cover and marinate in the fridge for at least 1/2 hour and up to 4 hours.

3 Heat a grill or grill pan to medium-high heat. Remove the chicken from its marinade (discard the marinade) and grill the chicken, turning once, until charred on both sides and cooked through, about 5 minutes per side.

4 Allow the chicken to rest for 5 minutes, then slice it crosswise into thin strips. Place the sliced chicken on a plate and pour the reserved marinade over it, turning to coat it evenly.

5 Serve hot or let cool and store in an airtight container in the fridge for up to 4 days.

CHICKEN TINGA

Pulled chicken is one of my favorite ways to eat chicken, especially if it is made with thighs. Chicken tinga—a Mexican pulled chicken dish typically flavored with tomato, onion, and smoky chipotle—originated in the Mexican state of Puebla (the birthplace of so many incredible dishes, including mole poblano) and is a staple in tacos, empanadas, tostadas, and more. My take on the dish is great on nachos, too (natch). It is so tender and flavorful, and the sauce really permeates the chicken—the opposite of a thick, dry chicken breast that is seasoned on the outside but bland in the center.

1 Heat the vegetable oil in a large heavy-bottomed pot over high heat. Add the chicken and cook, turning once, until browned on both sides, about 3 minutes per side.

2 Add the onion and cook, stirring often, until it begins to soften, about 5 minutes. Season the onion and chicken with the salt and pepper to taste.

3 Reduce the heat to medium and add the garlic. Cook until fragrant, about 1 minute. Add the tomato paste and cook, stirring, for about 3 minutes.

4 Add the vinegar, scraping the bottom of the pan to collect any browned bits, then add the beer, oregano, cumin, and chipotles and adobo sauce. Stir to combine and reduce the heat to low. Cover and simmer, stirring occasionally, until the chicken is tender and falling apart (it should shred apart as you stir it), about 90 minutes.

5 Remove from the heat and serve or let cool and store in an airtight container in the fridge for up to 5 days.

MAKES ABOUT 2 CUPS (ENOUGH FOR 1 BATCH OF NACHOS)

Takes about 2 hours

2 tablespoons vegetable oil

1½ pounds boneless, skinless chicken thighs

½ large yellow onion, peeled and diced

Kosher salt

Freshly cracked black pepper

2 cloves garlic, peeled and minced

1 can (6 ounces) tomato paste

¼ cup red wine vinegar

1 can (12 ounces) beer or 1½ cups chicken stock

1 teaspoon dried oregano flakes

1 tablespoon ground cumin

2 canned chipotle chiles in adobo, diced, plus 1 tablespoon adobo sauce from the can

CILANTRO LIME SHRIMP

I prefer refreshing shrimp recipes over heavy ones, so I wanted to make sure to include a bright citrusy shrimp for nachos. Shrimp cooks so quickly, I usually just salt it, cook it, and then dress it after.

MAKES ABOUT ¾ POUND COOKED SHRIMP (ENOUGH FOR 1 BATCH OF NACHOS)

Takes about 15 minutes

1 Season the shrimp with the salt and pepper.

2 Heat the oil in a large frying pan over medium-high heat. Add the shrimp and cook until they are starting to curl and become opaque, 2 to 3 minutes. Flip the shrimp with a spatula and cook until fully opaque, about 1 more minute.

3 Add the garlic and chili powder and cook, tossing the shrimp in the pan to coat, until the garlic is fragrant, about 1 minute. Remove from the heat and pour into a large bowl.

4 Add the lime juice to the shrimp in the bowl and toss to coat. Allow to cool for about 10 minutes, then add the cilantro and stir to combine.

5 Serve warm or store in an airtight container in the fridge for up to 3 days.

1 pound shrimp, peeled, deveined, and tails removed

1 teaspoon kosher salt

1 teaspoon freshly cracked black pepper

1 tablespoon olive oil

1 clove garlic, peeled and minced

1 teaspoon chili powder

Juice of 2 limes

¼ cup chopped fresh cilantro

NACHO INSPO!

▶ Surf and Turf: Top chips with this shrimp, Carne Asada (page 55), Chihuahua cheese, and Cotija cheese before baking, then top with Corn Salsa (page 18), Pico de Gallo (page 14), and Power Crema (page 36).

CRISPY COD

**MAKES 3 COD FILLETS
(ENOUGH FOR 1 BATCH
OF NACHOS)**

Takes about 15 minutes

2 tablespoons vegetable oil

1 cup buttermilk

1 cup yellow cornmeal

¼ cup all-purpose flour

2 teaspoons chili powder

1 teaspoon kosher salt

3 cod fillets (1 pound total)

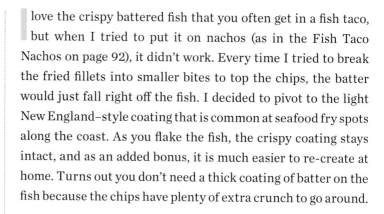

I love the crispy battered fish that you often get in a fish taco, but when I tried to put it on nachos (as in the Fish Taco Nachos on page 92), it didn't work. Every time I tried to break the fried fillets into smaller bites to top the chips, the batter would just fall right off the fish. I decided to pivot to the light New England–style coating that is common at seafood fry spots along the coast. As you flake the fish, the crispy coating stays intact, and as an added bonus, it is much easier to re-create at home. Turns out you don't need a thick coating of batter on the fish because the chips have plenty of extra crunch to go around.

1 Heat the oil in a large heavy-bottomed frying pan over medium-high heat.

2 Pour the buttermilk into a shallow bowl or baking dish. Stir together the flours, chili powder, and salt in a large bowl.

3 Pat the cod dry with paper towels, then dip the fillets into the buttermilk to coat. Next, dredge the cod in the flour mixture to coat. Use your hands to help press the coating onto the fish.

4 When the oil is hot and shimmering on the bottom of the pan, add the fish to the frying pan and cook until the coating is brown and crispy on the bottom, about 3 minutes. Gently turn the fish with a spatula and cook until it's flaky, opaque in the center, and browned on the other side, 3 to 5 more minutes.

5 Remove the fish from the pan and allow to cool on a wire rack or paper towel.

6 Serve hot. If using immediately on nachos, flake it apart into bite-size chunks. Otherwise, let it cool and store it in an airtight container in the fridge for up to 1 day. To reheat and re-crisp it, place it on a sheet pan and bake at 450°F for about 5 minutes.

BAKED SMOKY HONEY MUSTARD SALMON

Roasting salmon is one of the easiest things you can do in the kitchen, so it's a wonder to me that some people find it intimidating. This is one of my favorite ways to make it, but with a little smoky kick added for ideal nacho compatibility.

1 Preheat the oven to 400°F.

2 Stir together the mustard, honey, chipotle powder, and garlic powder in a small bowl.

3 Place the salmon on a sheet pan and season on both sides with the salt. Spread the mustard mixture over the top and sides of the fillets to coat evenly.

4 Bake until the salmon is opaque in the center and the mustard mixture has browned, 10 to 12 minutes.

5 Remove the salmon from the oven and let cool slightly. Serve warm. If using immediately on nachos, flake it apart into bite-size chunks before using on nachos. Otherwise, let it cool and store it whole in an airtight container in the fridge for up to 1 day. To reheat it, warm it in a small pan over low heat.

MAKES 3 SALMON FILLETS (ENOUGH FOR 1 BATCH OF NACHOS)
Takes about 20 minutes

½ cup Dijon mustard

2 tablespoons honey

1 teaspoon chipotle powder

1 teaspoon garlic powder

3 skinless salmon fillets
  (1 pound total)

¼ teaspoon kosher salt

NACHO INSPO!

▶ Baked Smoky Honey Mustard Salmon, Corn Salsa (page 18), and a little Cotija cheese, topped with Power Crema (page 36) and chopped dill

▶ Baked Smoky Honey Mustard Salmon, Cumin-Roasted Cauliflower (page 47), and shredded cheddar, topped with BLT Guac (page 32)

RAW FISH

Raw fish goes great with tortilla chips; it's actually one of the first ways I ever was brave enough to taste raw fish when I was younger and scared of good food. Young Dan said no to raw fish but couldn't say no to nachos.

Ceviche is a refreshing cold seafood dish that originated in Peru. It is practically salsa with fish in it and feels like a natural with tortilla chips. A good ceviche is bright and fresh and will wake you up when you take a bite!

Poke is a Hawaiian tradition that has become really trendy on the mainland United States in recent years. Where ceviche brings strong acidity and heat, poke brings mouth-coating oil, umami, and sweetness. The flavors and textures work great on crunchy chips, and poke tacos, burritos, and nachos have been appearing on menus everywhere!

In developing the recipes for this book, I was surprised to find that the lighter and more refreshing nachos rose to the top as my favorites—any version you make with ceviche or poke will be exactly that.

TUNA POKE

**MAKES ½ POUND
(ENOUGH FOR 1 BATCH
OF NACHOS)**

*Takes about 10 minutes,
plus 1 hour of rest*

½ pound sushi-grade bluefin
tuna, diced (see Note)

1 tablespoon toasted sesame
oil

1 teaspoon sesame seeds

1 teaspoon soy sauce

1 teaspoon crushed red pepper
flakes

3 scallions, trimmed and green
and white parts sliced

1 clove garlic, peeled and
grated

1 teaspoon rice vinegar

Kosher salt

NACHO INSPO!

NO-BAKE EDITION!
▶ Top tortilla chips with
Tuna Poke, thinly sliced
cucumbers, avocado
chunks, and Lime Crema
(page 35).

Combine the tuna, sesame oil, sesame seeds, soy sauce, red pepper flakes, scallions, garlic, and vinegar in a medium-size bowl. Add a few pinches of salt and stir to coat. Transfer to the fridge and let sit for the flavors to come together, about 1 hour. It's best eaten right away but will keep in an airtight container in the fridge for up to 2 days.

NOTE: Sushi-grade tuna is technically flash-frozen and then thawed as a way to kill anything that might be harmful on the fish. I usually buy mine fresh at the Korean grocery store near me, but I have also seen it at a handful of stores in the freezer. It usually comes with the skin and bones already removed, but if not, ask your fishmonger to remove them.

HALIBUT-MANGO CEVICHE

Combine the halibut, citrus juices, mango, onion, habanero, and garlic in a medium-size bowl. Add a few pinches of salt and stir to coat. Transfer to the fridge and let sit for the flavors to come together, 30 minutes to 1 hour, but no more than that. Serve immediately.

MAKES ½ POUND (ENOUGH FOR 1 BATCH OF NACHOS)
Takes about 10 minutes, plus 30 minutes of rest

½ pound halibut, deboned and skinned, diced (cod or any mild white fish will work here—freshness is key!)

¾ cup fresh lime juice (from 6 to 8 limes)

Juice of 1 orange

1 large ripe mango, peeled, pitted, and diced

½ small red onion, peeled and minced

1 habanero, stemmed, seeded, and minced

1 clove garlic, peeled and grated

Kosher salt

NACHO INSPO!

NO-BAKE EDITION!
▶ Top tortilla chips with ceviche, diced roasted sweet potato, corn nuts, and Guasacaca (page 34).

BURRITO INTERLUDE

The preceding recipes are pretty much the best burrito fillings ever—disguised as nacho toppings. You could mix and match them—following my suggestions below or using your own taste and imagination—to make a killer burrito. The only things missing are the tortilla and the rice! For the latter, simply steam or boil some rice—I like white or brown basmati—and then stir in the juice of a lime and a few tablespoons of chopped fresh cilantro. Now, let's make some burritos.

BURRITO STYLE	Cooked Grain	Bean	Proteins	Fresh Salsa	Hot Sauce	Creamy Topping	Cheese/ Toppings
MY NEVER-FAIL BURRITO ORDER	White rice	Meaty Pinto Beans (page 39)	Carnitas (page 50)	Pico de Gallo (page 14)	Honey Chipotle Sauce (page 21)	Lime Crema (page 35)	Jack cheese
SURF AND TURF	White rice	Basic Black Beans (page 38)	Cilantro Lime Shrimp (page 61) Carne Asada (page 55)	Mango Salsa (page 15)	Habanana Sauce (page 21)	Power Crema (page 36)	Shredded lettuce
SOUTH-WESTERN	White rice	Basic Black Beans (page 38)	Chili-Lime Grilled Chicken (page 58)	Pico de Gallo (page 14) Corn Salsa (page 18)	•••	Herby Crema (page 37)	Jack cheese
EARTHY CRUNCHY	Brown rice	Refried Beans (page 40)	Red Curry Chickpeas (page 41)	Cantaloupe Cucumber Salsa (page 17)	Guasacaca (page 34)	Vegan Crema (page 37)	Jicama Slaw (page 25)
SPICY-SWEET	White rice	Meaty Pinto Beans (page 39)	Mexican-Style Chorizo (page 54)	•••	Peach Habanero Salsa (page 16)	Herby Crema (page 37)	Pepper Jack cheese
POKE BOWL-RITO	White rice	Shelled edamame	Tuna Poke (page 66)	Cantaloupe Cucumber Salsa (page 17)	Honey Chipotle Sauce (page 21)	•••	Scallions, shredded lettuce, sliced avocado

PUTTING IT ALL TOGETHER:
CLASSIC NACHOS

This is the best version of what you'd get when ordering nachos at a restaurant. All the essential, irresistible components are here: Chips, cheese, meat, salsa, guac, and sour cream.

I make these on a sheet pan to maximize topping distribution, balance melty and crispy browned cheeses, and minimize naked chips. I also put the toppings right on the chips, but I make sure they're evenly spread out to avoid the dreaded glob that sits only on the first layer. Nothing challenges a friendship more than poorly distributed nacho toppings.

1 Preheat the broiler to low with a rack about 4 inches from the heat.

2 Spread the tortilla chips on a sheet pan in a single layer.

3 Sprinkle the Jack cheese on the chips, making sure to distribute it evenly, then top with the beef, using a spoon to dollop it on. Sprinkle the cheddar cheese over the top.

4 Broil until the cheese is melted and the chips are starting to brown at the edges, 3 to 5 minutes. (Watch carefully to make sure they don't burn.)

5 Remove from the oven and serve hot, with the pico, guac, and crema either dolloped on top or in small bowls on the side.

MAKES 4 SERVINGS FOR DINNER, OR 8 AS AN APPETIZER

Takes about 20 minutes

1 bag (12 ounces) tortilla chips (about 90 chips)

1½ cups (6 ounces) shredded Jack cheese

2 cups Taco-Style Ground Beef (page 49), at room temperature or warmer

1½ cups (6 ounces) shredded cheddar cheese

1 cup Pico de Gallo (store-bought or homemade; see page 14)

1 cup Guacamole (store-bought or homemade; see page 31)

½ cup sour cream or Lime Crema (page 35)

THE BALANCE SHEET (OF NACHOS)

NACHO STYLE	HOT		COLD	
	Deep Flavors/ Chewy Texture	Melty/Salty	Fresh/Slightly Sweet	Tart/Spicy/ Creamy
THE CLASSIC	Taco-Style Ground Beef (page 49)	Cheddar cheese, Jack cheese	Pico de Gallo (page 14)	Pickled jalapeños (store-bought or homemade; see page 29)
SOCAL	Carne Asada (page 55)	Cheddar cheese, Jack cheese	Guacamole (page 31)	Fresh lime wedges (for squeezing), sour cream
HERBED CAULIFLOWER	Cumin-Roasted Cauliflower (page 47)	Swiss cheese	Chimichurri (page 24)	Jicama Slaw (page 25)
WARMING COMFORT	Carnitas (page 50)	Roasted squash, Manchego cheese	Green Tomatillo Salsa (page 23)	Honey Chipotle Sauce (page 21)
SPICY-SWEET	Jalapeño Margarita Glazed Tofu (page 48)	Braised Cabbage (page 45), Jack cheese	Cantaloupe Cucumber Salsa (page 17)	Avocado Crema (page 36)
COWBOY CAVIAR	Meaty Pinto Beans (page 39)	Jack cheese, Cotija cheese	Corn Salsa (page 18) Pico de Gallo (page 14)	Avocado Crema (page 36)

SOUPS, SALADS, APPS—NACHOFIED

STREET CORN NACHOS

My personal opinion on street corn is this: Nine out of ten times, the corn tastes better *off* the cob. When you have a nice big bowl of perfectly balanced street corn, there is nothing getting in the way of shoveling it into your *face*.

That's why these street corn nachos, inspired by Mexican elote—the famous grilled corn topped with a mayo mixture, spices, and cheese—are great. Every bite has tons of corn and the perfect ratio of crema, cheese, corn, chips, and cilantro. If you make this in the summer, you can cut the corn off fresh in-season cobs. The rest of the year, frozen works just as well.

MAKES 4 SERVINGS
FOR DINNER, OR
8 AS AN APPETIZER
Takes about 20 minutes

3 cups (24 ounces) fresh
   or frozen corn kernels
   (see Note, page 74)

2 tablespoons olive oil

1 cup Power Crema (page 36)

1 bag (12 ounces) tortilla chips
   (about 90 chips)

2½ cups (10 ounces) shredded
   cheddar cheese

½ cup (2 ounces) crumbled
   Cotija cheese

2 teaspoons smoked paprika

½ cup chopped fresh cilantro

Lime wedges, for serving

1 Preheat the broiler to low with a rack about 4 inches from the heat.

2 Place the corn on a sheet pan, drizzle with the olive oil, and toss to coat. Broil until the corn is slightly charred, 3 to 5 minutes. (Watch carefully to make sure it doesn't burn.) Remove from the oven and let cool for 2 minutes.

3 Stir ¼ cup of the crema into the corn.

4 Arrange the tortilla chips evenly on a sheet pan, overlapping them as little as possible.

5 Top with half of the cheddar cheese, followed by half of the Cotija cheese.

6 Add the corn mixture, distributing it evenly, then the remaining cheddar cheese and Cotija cheese.

7 Broil on low until the cheddar cheese has melted (the Cotija won't melt) and the chips are starting to brown, 3 to 5 minutes. (Watch carefully to make sure they don't burn.) Remove from the oven.

8 Top the nachos with the remaining crema, followed by the paprika and cilantro. Serve hot, with lime wedges on the side.

NOTE: If you're using fresh corn, you'll need 5 or 6 shucked ears for this. To cut the kernels off a cob, place a small bowl upside-down inside a large bowl, and set the base of an ear of corn on top of the small bowl. Holding the ear upright with one hand, use a sharp knife to cut down toward the small bowl, slicing off the kernels and collecting them in the large bowl. Repeat with the remaining ears.

SOUTHWESTERN CHICKEN NACHOS

This is what nachos are all about! Lots of colors, lots of flavors, lots of textures, lots of temperatures. I talk often about choosing your own nacho adventure, but the key to *good* nachos is always balance. Try to hit crunchy, creamy, and chewy textures; savory, tart, and spicy flavors; and hot and cold temperatures; and match deep flavors with bright and fresh ones. (See the table on page 70 for more about balancing nachos.)

1 Preheat the broiler to high with a rack about 4 inches from the heat.

2 Place the corn on a sheet pan and brush with the olive oil. Broil until the corn is slightly charred, 3 to 5 minutes. (Watch carefully to make sure it doesn't burn.) Remove from the oven.

3 Arrange the tortilla chips evenly on a sheet pan, overlapping them as little as possible.

4 Top evenly with the Jack cheese, then the chicken, beans, and corn. Top with the queso blanco cheese.

5 Broil until the Jack cheese has melted and the chips are starting to brown, about 5 minutes. (Watch carefully to make sure they don't burn.) Remove from the oven.

6 Top the nachos with the cilantro and pickled onion. Serve hot.

MAKES 4 SERVINGS FOR DINNER, OR 8 AS AN APPETIZER
Takes about 20 minutes

1 cup fresh or frozen corn kernels (see Note, page 74)

2 tablespoons olive oil

1 bag (12 ounces) tortilla chips (about 90 chips)

1 cup (4 ounces) shredded Jack cheese

½ cup chopped Chili-Lime Grilled Chicken (page 58) or other grilled chicken breast

½ cup cooked black beans (canned or homemade; see page 38)

1 cup (4 ounces) crumbled queso blanco cheese

¼ cup fresh cilantro

2 tablespoons pickled onion (store-bought or homemade; see page 28)

CAPRESE NACHOS

**MAKES 4 SERVINGS
FOR DINNER, OR
8 AS AN APPETIZER**

Takes about 15 minutes

1 bag (12 ounces) tortilla chips
(about 90 chips)

1½ cups (6 ounces) shredded
low-moisture mozzarella
cheese

2 cups roughly chopped
ripe heirloom tomatoes
(3 to 5 tomatoes)

½ cup grated Pecorino Romano
cheese

About 30 basil leaves, cut into
slivers, plus a few whole
leaves for garnish

¼ cup balsamic glaze
(see Note)

It's hard to beat the taste of lightly salted heirloom tomatoes in August with a touch of fresh mozzarella and basil—but topping tortilla chips with this mixture is pretty darn good, too. Some might think it's a travesty to cook perfectly ripe heirlooms, but we are really just warming them up—and the little bit of heat concentrates that beautiful summertime flavor. (As an added bonus, you can make this at other times of year—the slight cooking gives off-season tomatoes a flavor boost.)

1 Preheat the broiler to low with a rack about 4 inches from the heat.

2 Arrange the tortilla chips evenly on a sheet pan, overlapping them as little as possible.

3 Sprinkle the mozzarella cheese over the top, then the tomatoes, and finally the Pecorino Romano cheese.

4 Broil until the cheeses have melted and the chips are starting to brown, 3 to 5 minutes. (Watch carefully to make sure they don't burn.) Remove from the oven.

5 Top the nachos with the basil. Drizzle on the balsamic glaze and serve hot.

NOTE: Balsamic glaze is available at most supermarkets (it's also sold as balsamic syrup or reduction). If you can't find it, it's simple enough to make your own: Heat 1 cup of balsamic vinegar (plus 1 tablespoon of brown sugar if you want it sweeter) in a saucepan over medium-low heat until it comes to a very low simmer. Cook until it has thickened enough to coat the back of a spoon and reduced to ¼ cup, about 1 hour.

COBB SALAD NACHOS

When I set out to nachofy a Cobb salad, I was a little worried about topping chips with hard-boiled egg—would it be good? But the classic Cobb combo didn't let me down. How could a combination of rich hard-boiled eggs, crispy bacon, creamy avocado, and cool tomato *not* be good? The essential nacho interplay of cold and hot ingredients is really on display here!

MAKES 4 SERVINGS
FOR DINNER, OR
8 AS AN APPETIZER
Takes about 20 minutes

1 bag (12 ounces) tortilla chips (about 90 chips)

1½ cups (6 ounces) shredded Jack cheese

5 slices bacon, cooked and crumbled

1 cup chopped Chili-Lime Grilled Chicken (page 58)

10 cherry tomatoes, quartered

¾ cup (3 ounces) crumbled blue cheese

2 large hard-boiled eggs, peeled and diced

1 ripe avocado, pitted, peeled, and diced

1 Preheat the broiler to low with a rack about 4 inches from the heat.

2 Arrange the tortilla chips evenly on a sheet pan, overlapping them as little as possible.

3 Top the chips evenly with the Jack cheese. Next sprinkle on the bacon, then the chicken, and then the tomatoes. Finally, top with the blue cheese.

4 Broil until the Jack cheese has melted, the blue cheese has softened, and the chips are starting to brown, 3 to 5 minutes. (Watch carefully to make sure they don't burn.)

5 Remove from the oven and top the nachos with the eggs and avocado. Serve hot.

SPINACH ARTICHOKE DIPCHOS

**MAKES 4 SERVINGS
FOR DINNER, OR
8 AS AN APPETIZER**

Takes about 20 minutes

1 block (8 ounces) cream
cheese, at room temperature

¼ cup sour cream

¼ cup mayo

2 cloves garlic, peeled and
grated

Juice of 1 lemon

½ teaspoon kosher salt

10 ounces frozen chopped
spinach, thawed

1 bag (12 ounces) tortilla chips
(about 90 chips)

1 can (14 ounces) artichoke
hearts, drained and roughly
chopped

2 cups (8 ounces) shredded
low-moisture mozzarella
cheese

½ cup grated Parmesan cheese

While it might be fine simply to heap spinach artichoke dip
onto some tortilla chips and call it a day, I prefer to break
the creamy, hearty dip into its component parts first. This
really highlights each ingredient, reminding you of what you
loved about spinach artichoke dip the first time you tried it.

1 Mix together the cream cheese, sour cream, mayo, garlic,
lemon juice, and salt in a small bowl or food processor.
Set aside.

2 Wrap the thawed spinach in a paper towel or kitchen towel
and squeeze to remove excess moisture.

3 Preheat the broiler to low with a rack about 4 inches from
the heat.

4 Arrange the tortilla chips evenly on a sheet pan, overlapping
them as little as possible.

5 Drizzle the cream cheese sauce evenly over the chips. The
sauce will be slightly thick, so a squeeze bottle will help.
Top with the artichoke hearts, followed by the spinach,
spreading both as evenly as possible to cover all the chips.
Top with the mozzarella and Parmesan cheeses.

6 Broil until the cheeses have melted and the chips are
starting to brown, 3 to 5 minutes. (Watch carefully to make
sure they don't burn.)

7 Remove from the oven and serve hot.

FRENCH ONION SOUPCHOS

French onion soup is the king of all apps, and all of the ingredients except the broth itself are very nacho-ready. If you think about it, it's the nacho of soups, 'cause you melt the cheese directly on top of it! All of the flavor for the soup comes from deeply caramelized onions, so here you can just skip the broth and put those concentrated onion flavors right on the chips. I debated whether the croutons were too much carb-on-carb overkill, but the true essence of the soup is lost without them.

1 Melt the butter in a large frying pan over medium-low heat. Add the onions and salt and cook, stirring occasionally, until the onions are a deep brown, about 45 minutes.

2 Stir in the vinegar and thyme and cook until the vinegar is absorbed, about 3 minutes. Remove from the heat.

3 Preheat the broiler to low with a rack about 4 inches from the heat.

4 Arrange the tortilla chips evenly on a sheet pan, overlapping them as little as possible.

5 Sprinkle 1 cup of the cheese on the chips, distributing it evenly. Next, add the onions and croutons. Top with the remaining cheese.

6 Broil until the cheese has melted and the chips are starting to brown, 3 to 5 minutes. (Watch carefully to make sure they don't burn.)

7 Remove from the oven and serve hot.

MAKES 4 SERVINGS FOR DINNER, OR 8 AS AN APPETIZER

Takes about 1 hour

4 tablespoons (½ stick) unsalted butter

4 large yellow onions, peeled and sliced into ¼-inch rounds

½ teaspoon kosher salt

1 tablespoon red wine vinegar

1 teaspoon fresh thyme

1 bag (12 ounces) tortilla chips (about 90 chips)

3 cups (12 ounces) grated Gruyère cheese

2 cups croutons

CHEESY BACON POTATO CHIPCHOS

MAKES 4 SERVINGS FOR DINNER, OR 8 AS AN APPETIZER

Takes about 15 minutes

1 bag (14 ounces) crinkle-cut potato chips

1 cup Nacho Cheese Sauce (page 7)

½ pound bacon, cooked until crisp, then crumbled

3 scallions, trimmed and green and white parts thinly sliced

½ cup Lime Crema (page 35)

My first potato chip nacho experience was at an Irish pub, MJ O'Connor's, in Boston, where they were billed as "Irish nachos." Potato chips tend to be more fragile than tortilla chips, so I expected a big mess on a plate. I was wrong. Turns out that using sturdy crinkle-cut chips and drizzling them with cheese sauce is a winning combo. This is my take on them. I top these with crispy bacon, which is how I usually see them served, but if you substitute (or add!) leftover corned beef, that will really put these over the top.

This is a less substantial nachos-for-dinner situation than some of the other dishes in this book, so I serve it with a nice big kale salad. Life is about balance, right?

1 Arrange the potato chips evenly on a sheet pan, overlapping them as little as possible.

2 Drizzle half of the cheese sauce over the chips, distributing it evenly. Top with the bacon and half of the scallions, then the remaining cheese sauce.

3 Drizzle on the crema and sprinkle on the remaining scallions. Serve immediately.

BUFFALO CHICKEN NACHOS

**MAKES 4 SERVINGS
FOR DINNER, OR
8 AS AN APPETIZER**

Takes about 35 minutes

3 tablespoons unsalted butter

1 pound boneless, skinless
chicken breasts, thinly sliced

¼ teaspoon kosher salt

¼ teaspoon freshly cracked
black pepper

¼ cup cayenne hot sauce
(such as Frank's RedHot or
Crystal)

1 teaspoon smoked paprika

1 bag (12 ounces) tortilla chips
(about 90 chips)

2 cups (8 ounces) shredded
cheddar cheese

½ cup diced carrot

½ cup diced celery

½ cup (2 ounces) crumbled
blue cheese

½ cup of your favorite ranch
dressing or Herby Crema
(page 37)

Buffalo chicken nachos are a staple in bars, and I am here for it. In my take on this popular pub grub, I simmer the chicken in butter and hot sauce instead of frying it to save some effort, plus the chips are already doing a good job of providing crunch to the equation. Celery and carrot are just as integral to buffalo chicken as the chicken itself, so we'll add some on top with the blue cheese (they don't cook much, but if you prefer them totally raw, you can toss them on at the very end).

1 Melt the butter in a large frying pan over medium-high heat.

2 Add the chicken and season with the salt and pepper.

3 Cook the chicken until browned on the bottom, about 3 minutes. Flip with a spatula or tongs and add the hot sauce and paprika. Continue cooking, stirring occasionally, until cooked through, about 3 minutes. Remove from the heat.

4 Transfer the chicken to a cutting board (leave the sauce in the pan) and chop it into small pieces. Return it to the pan and stir to coat it in the sauce.

5 Preheat the broiler to low with a rack about 4 inches from the heat.

6 Arrange the tortilla chips evenly on a sheet pan, overlapping them as little as possible.

7 Sprinkle 1 cup of the cheddar cheese on the chips, distributing it evenly. Next add the chicken, carrot, and celery. Top with the remaining cheddar cheese and then the blue cheese.

8 Broil until the cheddar cheese has melted and the chips are starting to brown, 3 to 5 minutes. (Watch carefully to make sure they don't burn.)

9 Remove the nachos from the oven. Drizzle on the ranch dressing and serve hot.

CHICKEN LARB NACHOS

old nachos? With *no* cheese? Controversial! But let me tell you—when I put these down on the table in front of some friends, who were hanging out on my roof deck on a warm evening, all doubts melted away like coconut cream over chicken larb. These are flavor-charged nachos! Larb is one of my favorite Thai dishes because of its vibrant, refreshing flavor, so it fits perfectly with tortilla chips in the same way a fresh salsa would. Coconut isn't traditionally served with larb, but I added it to these nachos as a sour cream substitute—and it works!

Larb was one of the first things I ate at a Thai restaurant that wasn't Americanized pad Thai or one of the rainbow curries, and it opened my eyes to the vibrant, amazing flavors of true Thai cuisine. If you want to learn more about larb and other Thai dishes and cooking techniques, check out the cookbooks by Leela Punyaratabandhu or her website, SheSimmers.com.

MAKES 4 SERVINGS FOR DINNER, OR 8 AS AN APPETIZER
Takes about 45 minutes

1 tablespoon olive oil

½ pound ground chicken

½ tablespoon fish sauce (or soy sauce if allergic or averse to fish sauce), plus extra as needed

2 tablespoons fresh lime juice (from 1 lime), plus extra as needed

2 tablespoons sambal chili paste

1 teaspoon honey

1 shallot, peeled and sliced into ¼-inch rounds

½ cup canned coconut milk

½ English cucumber, diced (1 cup)

1 tablespoon soy sauce

About 20 leaves fresh mint, ½ finely chopped, ½ ripped into large pieces

1 bag (12 ounces) tortilla chips (about 90 chips)

1 Heat the olive oil in a large frying pan over medium-high heat. Add the chicken and cook, stirring occasionally, until cooked through and lightly browned, about 7 minutes. Remove from the heat.

2 Transfer the chicken to a medium-size mixing bowl. Add the fish sauce, the lime juice, 1 tablespoon of chili paste, the honey, and the shallot and stir to combine. Cover and refrigerate for 30 minutes.

3 Meanwhile, stir together the coconut milk, cucumber, soy sauce, and remaining tablespoon of chili paste until incorporated. Cover and store in the fridge until ready to use.

4 Remove the chicken from the fridge and stir in the chopped mint to combine. Taste and adjust the seasonings, adding more lime juice and fish sauce if needed.

5 Arrange the tortilla chips evenly on a sheet pan or large platter, overlapping them as little as possible.

6 Distribute the chicken evenly among the chips. Drizzle the sauce over the top, add the ripped mint leaves, and serve.

SCALLION PANCAKE NACHOS

MAKES 4 SERVINGS FOR DINNER, OR 8 AS AN APPETIZER

Takes about 1 hour

1 pound boneless pork spareribs

1 tablespoon grated ginger

1 tablespoon grated garlic

1 teaspoon five-spice powder

2 teaspoons sweet paprika

2 tablespoons soy sauce

1 tablespoon rice vinegar

2 teaspoons sambal chili paste

2 teaspoons honey

2 tablespoons vegetable oil, plus extra as needed

14 ounces frozen scallion pancakes (4 or 5 whole pancakes to make about 30 wedges)

2 cups (8 ounces) shredded Jack cheese

½ cup pickled jalapeño slices (store-bought or homemade; see page 29)

After ordering Chinese takeout and having some scallion pancakes that were much crispier than normal, I decided to give scallion pancakes a try as nachos. I fried up wedges of the pancakes to make them extra crispy, then topped them with boneless spareribs, pickled jalapeños, and lots of cheese. I love making my own scallion pancakes from scratch, but for this recipe I suggest finding some in the freezer section or ordering extra with your next takeout. Almost as delicious and much easier!

1 Place the pork in a large bowl. Add the ginger, garlic, five-spice powder, paprika, soy sauce, vinegar, chili paste, and honey and stir to combine and coat.

2 Transfer the pork and its sauce to a large frying pan over medium heat. Bring to a simmer, then reduce the heat to low. Cook, stirring occasionally, until the sauce has thickened and the meat is tender but still has some chew to it, about 20 minutes. Transfer to a cutting board and let cool for 5 minutes, pouring any excess sauce into a large bowl. Cut the spareribs into bite-size pieces and toss them in the bowl with the sauce.

3 Heat the vegetable oil in a large frying pan. When it is hot, add the scallion pancakes in a single layer, working in batches so you don't crowd the pan, and cook, adding more

oil as needed, until they are browned and crispy (this will be a few minutes longer than directed on the package). Transfer the cooked pancakes to a paper towel–lined cutting board to cool.

4 Preheat the broiler to low with a rack about 4 inches from the heat.

5 Cut the cooled scallion pancakes into tortilla chip–size triangles and arrange them evenly on a sheet pan, overlapping them as little as possible.

6 Sprinkle half of the cheese on the chips, distributing it evenly. Then add the jalapeños and pork, and finally the remaining cheese.

7 Broil until the cheese has melted and the pancakes are starting to brown, 3 to 5 minutes. (Watch carefully to make sure they don't burn.) Remove from the oven and serve hot.

PLANTAIN NACHOS
WITH CARNITAS AND BLACK BEANS

Fried plantains really give these nachos a unique yet familiar flavor. These are some of the heartiest and most filling nachos I have had. A store near me sells sturdy plantain strips that are nice and long, making them perfect vehicles for nacho toppings. (The round kind are generally too small to hold all the ingredients, resulting in an unbalanced bite.) If you can't find long plantain strips at a store near you, I suggest looking online.

**MAKES 4 SERVINGS
FOR DINNER, OR
8 AS AN APPETIZER**

Takes about 15 minutes

1 bag (12 ounces) plantain
strips (about 80 strips)

1½ cups (6 ounces) shredded
cheddar cheese

1½ cups carnitas
(preferably homemade;
see page 50)

1 cup cooked black beans
(canned or homemade;
see page 38)

1½ cups (6 ounces) shredded
Chihuahua cheese

½ cup Lime Crema (page 35)

¼ cup Habanana Sauce
(page 21)

1 ripe avocado, pitted, peeled,
and thinly sliced

1 lime, quartered and sliced
into small wedges

1 Preheat the broiler to low with a rack about 4 inches from
the heat.

2 Arrange the plaintain chips evenly on a sheet pan,
overlapping them as little as possible.

3 Sprinkle the cheddar cheese on the chips, distributing it
evenly. Next add the carnitas, then the beans, and top with
the Chihuahua cheese.

4 Broil until the cheese has melted and the chips are starting
to brown, 3 to 5 minutes. (Watch carefully to make sure they
don't burn.) Remove from the oven.

5 Drizzle the crema and hot sauce on the nachos and top with
the avocado and lime wedges. Serve hot.

SANDWICHES AND TACOS (BUT MAKE THEM NACHOS)

FISH TACO NACHOS

MAKES 4 SERVINGS
FOR DINNER, OR
8 AS AN APPETIZER

Takes about 1 hour

1 bag (12 ounces) tortilla chips
(about 90 chips)

1 cup (4 ounces) shredded
Jack cheese

¼ cup (2 ounces) crumbled
Cotija cheese

1 batch Crispy Cod (page 62),
or 3 store-bought breaded
fish fillets, flaked

1 cup Creamy Crunchy Slaw
(page 26)

¼ cup fresh cilantro

¼ cup Lime Crema (page 35)

2 tablespoons chipotle sauce
(store-bought or homemade;
see page 21)

When made right, fish tacos are so fresh, crunchy, creamy, and bright—possibly the absolute best a taco can be. What a coincidence that these are all attributes I look for in a plate of nachos! I wanted to make sure to capture the true essence of these tacos in nacho form, so I went light on the cheese and topped them with refreshing, zesty slaw and lots of cilantro.

1 Preheat the broiler to high with a rack about 4 inches from the heat.

2 Arrange the tortilla chips evenly on a sheet pan, overlapping them as little as possible.

3 Sprinkle the Jack cheese on the chips, distributing it evenly. Next add the Cotija cheese, followed by the cod.

4 Broil until the cheese has melted and the chips are starting to brown, about 5 minutes. (Watch carefully to make sure they don't burn.) Remove from the oven.

5 Top the nachos with the slaw, cilantro, crema, and chipotle sauce. Serve hot.

LOBSTER NACHOS

MAKES 4 SERVINGS
FOR DINNER, OR
8 AS AN APPETIZER

Takes about 30 minutes

3 tablespoons unsalted butter

1 pound cooked fresh lobster
meat, chopped into bite-size
chunks (from about 4 live
lobsters, 1 pound each)

½ teaspoon kosher salt

¼ teaspoon freshly cracked
black pepper

1 bag (12 ounces) tortilla chips
(about 90 chips)

1 cup (4 ounces) shredded
cheddar cheese

1 cup (4 ounces) grated Jack
cheese

½ cup Power Crema (page 36)

½ cup Guasacaca (page 34)

¼ cup chopped fresh chives

I'm not sure why lobster nachos aren't more popular, especially given the success of lobster mac and cheese. People are often afraid to pair cheese and seafood, but with a light touch, it can be a great combination! I like to use mild cheddar cheese for these nachos so the sharpness of the cheese doesn't overpower the flavor of the lobster. I also cook the lobster in butter and use a mayo-based crema because butter and mayo are no strangers to lobster. Top with chives and an avocado sauce to add a little freshness.

1 Melt the butter in a large frying pan over medium-low heat. Add the lobster and season with the salt and pepper. Cook until warmed through, about 2 minutes. Set aside.

2 Preheat the broiler to high with a rack about 4 inches from the heat.

3 Arrange the tortilla chips evenly on a sheet pan, overlapping them as little as possible.

4 Sprinkle the cheddar cheese on the chips, distributing it evenly. Next add the lobster pieces and drizzle on their pan juices. Finally, add the Jack cheese.

5 Broil until the cheese has melted and the chips are starting to brown, about 5 minutes. (Watch carefully to make sure they don't burn.) Remove from the oven.

6 Drizzle the crema and guasacaca on the nachos (or serve them in bowls on the side if you prefer). Top with the chives and serve hot.

CHEESEBURGER NACHOS

What is burger flavor really? Ground beef, cheese, and bread at the baseline level. I like my burgers with pickles, onions, tomato, and Thousand Island dressing, so these nachos reflect that. Feel free to tinker with these nachos to include your favorite burger toppings!

MAKES 4 SERVINGS FOR DINNER, OR 8 AS AN APPETIZER

Takes about 30 minutes

1 teaspoon vegetable oil

½ pound ground beef (85% lean)

¾ teaspoon kosher salt

¾ teaspoon freshly cracked black pepper

1 cup mayo

¼ cup ketchup

2 tablespoons pickle relish

Juice of 1 lemon

1 teaspoon smoked paprika

1 bag (12 ounces) tortilla chips (about 90 chips)

6 slices (4 ounces) American cheese, torn into bite-size pieces

1 cup (4 ounces) shredded cheddar cheese

2 vine-ripened tomatoes, stemmed and diced

2 dill pickles, diced

¼ small white onion, peeled and diced

1 Heat the oil in a large frying pan over high heat. Add the ground beef and cook, stirring occasionally to break up the meat, until it is browned and cooked through, about 10 minutes. Season with the salt and pepper and stir to combine. Transfer the meat to a bowl, draining most of the fat.

2 Stir together the mayo, ketchup, relish, lemon juice, and paprika in a small bowl. Cover and refrigerate until ready to use.

3 Preheat the broiler to low with a rack about 4 inches from the heat.

4 Arrange the tortilla chips evenly on a sheet pan, overlapping them as little as possible.

5 Top the chips with the American cheese, distributing it evenly. Add the cooked beef, then top with the cheddar cheese.

6 Broil until the cheese has melted and the chips are starting to brown, 3 to 5 minutes. (Watch carefully to make sure they don't burn.) Remove from the oven.

7 Top the nachos with the tomatoes, pickles, and onion. Remove the sauce from the fridge and drizzle it on the nachos. Serve hot.

Variation

HOT DOG NACHOS: This is also great as a game-day hot dog nacho. Just replace the beef with 4 diced hot dogs and replace the Thousand Island dressing with mustard.

CHEESESTEAK NACHOS

Cheesesteak flavors lend themselves to nachos really well. The cheese can be a hot topic to cheesesteak purists—some say Cheez Whiz, others say provolone; some say mushrooms or peppers are acceptable, others *absolutely not*—so I tried to tread carefully with this recipe. We start with cheddar as a base and top the nachos with drippy Cheez Whiz to honor what some would argue adds that true Philly flavor (if you like, you can use the Nacho Cheese Sauce on page 7 instead). Caramelized onions are necessary for me in a cheesesteak, but I also love to add pickled peppers for a little brightness.

1 Melt the butter in a large frying pan over medium-high heat. Add the onions and stir to coat with the butter.

2 Cook the onions, adjusting the heat as needed—up if they aren't browning enough or down if onion bits start to burn on the bottom of the pan—until they are a deep brown and reduced in size, about 30 minutes. Remove from the pan and set aside.

3 Turn the heat up to high and add the steak to the pan (with the vegetable oil if needed). Season with salt and pepper. Cook, stirring often and using 2 spatulas to break up the meat, until browned and cooked through, about 10 minutes. Remove from the heat.

4 Preheat the broiler to high with a rack about 4 inches from the heat.

5 Meanwhile, gently warm the Cheez Whiz in a small saucepan over low heat or in a bowl in the microwave in 10-second increments.

6 Arrange the tortilla chips evenly on a sheet pan, overlapping them as little as possible.

MAKES 4 SERVINGS
FOR DINNER, OR
8 AS AN APPETIZER
Takes about 1 hour

2 tablespoons unsalted butter

2 large yellow onions, peeled and diced

1 pound shaved steak

1 tablespoon vegetable oil (optional)

Kosher salt and freshly cracked black pepper

1 cup Cheez Whiz

1 bag (12 ounces) tortilla chips (about 90 chips)

1½ cups (6 ounces) shredded cheddar cheese

½ cup pickled peppers slices (store-bought or homemade; see page 29)

7 Sprinkle the cheese on the chips, distributing it evenly. Next add the steak, followed by the onions and then the pickled peppers. Drizzle the Cheez Whiz over all.

8 Broil until the cheese has melted and the chips are starting to brown, 3 to 5 minutes. (Watch carefully to make sure they don't burn.) Remove from the oven. Serve hot.

SAUSAGE AND PEPPER NACHOS

**MAKES 4 SERVINGS
FOR DINNER, OR
8 AS AN APPETIZER**
Takes about 40 minutes

½ pound Italian sausage or bratwurst

1 tablespoon olive oil

1 red bell pepper, stemmed, seeded, and sliced into thin strips

1 green bell pepper, stemmed, seeded, and sliced into thin strips

1 large white onion, peeled and sliced into ½-inch rounds

1 bag (12 ounces) tortilla chips (about 90 chips)

6 slices (4 ounces) Swiss cheese, torn into bite-size pieces

2 cups (8 ounces) shredded cheddar cheese

¼ cup Dijon mustard

These nachos taste like going to a tailgate. The smell of cooking onions always reminds me of the first time I went to a baseball game. I love browned onions on pretty much anything, but they pair especially well with a game-day sausage. If you want to give these an Italian twist, like my mother used to do, try swapping out the mustard for marinara sauce.

1 Place 1 cup of water in a small frying pan and add the sausage. Bring to a simmer over medium heat and cook until the sausage starts to lose its pink color, about 5 minutes. Turn and cook on the other side until the sausage is cooked most of the way through, about 5 minutes. Drain the water from the pan and add the olive oil. Return the pan to the heat and continue to cook the sausage, turning, until browned on both sides and cooked through, about 5 minutes. Remove the sausage from the pan and set aside on a plate.

2 Add the bell peppers and onion to the pan and cook over medium heat until softened and browned slightly, 15 to 20 minutes.

3 Preheat the broiler to low with a rack about 4 inches from the heat.

4 Slice the sausage lengthwise into halves, then slice the halves crosswise into ½-inch-thick half-moons.

5 Arrange the tortilla chips evenly on a sheet pan, overlapping them as little as possible.

6 Top with the Swiss cheese, distributing it evenly. Next add the sausage, then the peppers and onion. Top with the cheddar cheese.

7 Broil until the cheese has melted and the chips are starting to brown, 3 to 5 minutes. (Watch carefully to make sure they don't burn.) Remove from the oven.

8 Drizzle the nachos with the mustard or put it on the side for dipping. Serve hot.

BANH MI NACHOS

I was lucky enough to grow up in a city with a substantial Vietnamese community: Springfield, Massachusetts. When I started cooking and wanted to explore new flavors, I would visit the tiny Vietnamese shops for flavors I couldn't find at the supermarket. At the checkout, many sold banh mi sandwiches, and I would grab one as a quick snack. If you follow my blog or have read my previous books, you know I love mash-ups. I didn't realize it at the time, but banh mi is actually a mash-up recipe: It traces its roots to the French occupation of Vietnam between 1887 and 1954, when the imperialists introduced French ingredients and cooking techniques to Vietnam. The sandwich combines crusty French bread, pâté, and mayo with Vietnamese-style pickles and pork marinated in fish sauce.

To nachofy banh mi, I went with a simple Vietnamese-inspired grilled pork and skipped the pâté; if you want to go all-in with traditional toppings, feel free to add chicken liver pâté to these. Either way, the pickled carrot and radish are

**MAKES 4 SERVINGS
FOR DINNER, OR
8 AS AN APPETIZER**

*Takes about 30 minutes, plus at
least 30 minutes for marinating*

1 pound boneless pork
  spareribs

2 tablespoons fish sauce
  (or soy sauce if allergic or
  averse to fish sauce)

1 teaspoon soy sauce

1 shallot, peeled and minced

1 tablespoon sugar

¼ teaspoon kosher salt

1 bag (12 ounces) tortilla chips
  (about 90 chips)

2 cups (8 ounces) shredded
  Jack cheese

1 cup pickled carrot and radish
  (store-bought or homemade;
  see page 28)

½ cup pickled jalapeño slices
  (store-bought or homemade;
  see page 29)

½ cup sriracha

½ cup Power Crema (page 36)

1 cup chopped fresh cilantro

absolutely critical—without them, these nachos just won't have
the right taste. If you like these nachos and are curious about
cooking Vietnamese recipes, dig deeper with books like *Street
Food Vietnam* by Jerry Mai or *Eat Real Vietnamese Food* by Lien
Nguyen.

1 Place the spareribs in a large bowl and add the fish sauce,
   soy sauce, shallot, sugar, and salt. Turn to coat. Cover and
   let marinate for 30 minutes on the counter or up to 8 hours
   in the fridge.

2 Preheat a grill or grill pan to medium-low heat. Place the
   spareribs on the grill and cook, turning often, until the fat
   is tender and the meat is lightly charred but not burned,
   about 20 minutes. (It can burn easily because of the sugar
   content in the marinade, so keep your eye on it and move it
   around on the grill for even charring.) Remove from the heat
   and let cool slightly on a cutting board. Chop the spareribs
   into bite-size pieces.

3 Preheat the broiler to low with a rack about 4 inches from
   the heat.

4 Arrange the tortilla chips evenly on a sheet pan, overlapping
   them as little as possible.

5 Sprinkle 1 cup of the cheese on the chips, distributing it
   evenly. Top with the chopped spareribs, then the remaining
   cheese.

6 Broil until the cheese has melted and the chips are starting
   to brown, 3 to 5 minutes. (Watch carefully to make sure they
   don't burn.) Remove from the oven.

7 Top the nachos with the pickled veggies, drizzle on the
   sriracha and crema, and top with the cilantro. Serve hot.

CUBANO NACHOS

I still remember the first time I had a Cubano sandwich and was confused about why there were hot pickles in my grilled cheese. What a sad, naive boy I was. Cubanos are one of my favorite sandwiches now, and the ingredients work so well in nachos! Ham, pork, and Swiss are obvious toppings for nachos, and if you have read this far, you have already seen that there are several recipes with pickles. The brightness of pickled ingredients always helps offset heavier ingredients like meat and cheese.

1 Combine the lime juice, orange juice, garlic, cumin, oregano, cloves, and salt in a shallow bowl. Add the pork chops and turn to coat. Cover and marinate for 1 hour at room temperature or as long as overnight in the fridge.

2 When ready to cook, heat the vegetable oil in a frying pan over medium-high heat. Add the pork chops to the pan, discarding the marinade. Cook, turning once, until browned and cooked through, 3 minutes per side. Transfer to a cutting board and allow to cool for 5 minutes. Chop the pork into thin bite-size pieces.

3 Preheat the broiler to low with a rack about 4 inches from the heat.

4 Arrange the tortilla chips evenly on a sheet pan, overlapping them as little as possible.

5 Sprinkle half of the cheese on the chips, distributing it evenly. Next, top with the chopped pork, ham, and pickles. Top with the remaining cheese.

6 Broil until the cheese has melted and the chips are starting to brown, 3 to 5 minutes. (Watch carefully to make sure they don't burn.) Remove from the oven.

7 Top the nachos with a drizzle of the mustard. Serve hot.

MAKES 4 SERVINGS FOR DINNER, OR 8 AS AN APPETIZER

Takes about 30 minutes, plus at least 1 hour for marinating

Juice of 1 lime

Juice of 1 orange

3 cloves garlic, peeled and grated

1 teaspoon ground cumin

1 teaspoon dried oregano flakes

Pinch of ground cloves

½ teaspoon kosher salt

½ pound thinly sliced boneless pork chops

1 tablespoon vegetable oil

1 bag (12 ounces) tortilla chips (about 90 chips)

2 cups (8 ounces) shredded Swiss cheese

5 slices (¼ pound) deli ham, chopped

2 dill pickles, diced

¼ cup yellow mustard

ITALIAN SUB NACHOS

**MAKES 4 SERVINGS
FOR DINNER, OR
8 AS AN APPETIZER**

Takes about 20 minutes

1 bag (12 ounces) tortilla chips
(about 90 chips)

2½ cups (10 ounces) shredded
"Italian blend" cheese

5 slices (¼ pound) mortadella,
chopped

10 slices (¼ pound) Genoa
salami, chopped

¼ cup diced jarred roasted
red pepper

1 romaine heart, trimmed and
shredded

¼ cup diced peperoncini
(from about 20 rings)

2 tablespoons olive oil

2 tablespoons balsamic vinegar

Pinch of kosher salt

A perfect Italian sub is one of my true weaknesses. The play among the salty meats, the thick, crusty bread that almost cuts your mouth as you eat it, and the crisp lettuce and bright peperoncini . . . my stomach is growling just thinking about it. These nachos are an ode to that amazing sandwich. Putting the meats and cheeses onto the chips seems like an obvious choice, but I feel particularly clever for making a little salad out of shredded romaine, peperoncini, olive oil, and balsamic vinegar and throwing that on top!

1 Preheat the broiler to low with a rack about 4 inches from the heat.

2 Arrange the tortilla chips evenly on a sheet pan, overlapping them as little as possible.

3 Sprinkle half of the cheese on the chips, distributing it evenly. Next, layer on the mortadella, salami, and red pepper. Top with the remaining cheese.

4 Broil the nachos on low until the cheese has melted and the chips are starting to brown, 3 to 5 minutes. (Watch carefully to make sure they don't burn.) Remove from the oven.

5 Meanwhile, combine the lettuce, peperoncini, oil, and vinegar in a large bowl. Season with the salt and toss to combine.

6 Top the nachos with the salad. Serve hot.

LAMB GYRO NACHOS

The Greek gyro sandwich—highly seasoned spit-roasted lamb or beef shaved onto a soft, fluffy, fresh-baked pita—takes its name from the Modern Greek word gyros, meaning "turn"—which is what the meat does as it cooks on the rotisserie. These nachos take the flavorings of a gyro but leave behind the spit—instead I mix all the seasonings into ground lamb for a similar effect. Pita chips work great as a tortilla chip replacement and are especially sturdy for a hearty nacho dish like this one. When that seasoned lamb comes together with the tzatziki and cucumber salad into one magical bite, the essence of a gyro is achieved.

1 Make the tzatziki sauce: Stir together the yogurt, cucumber, parsley, garlic, lemon juice, salt, and pepper in a small bowl to combine. Cover and store in the fridge until ready to use.

2 Make the nachos: Place the lamb in a large bowl and add the salt, pepper, onion, garlic, cumin, oregano, and rosemary. Stir to combine. Cover and allow to marinate in the fridge for 1 hour or as long as overnight.

3 Heat the oil in a large frying pan over medium-high heat, add the lamb, and cook, stirring occasionally, until starting to brown and render fat, about 5 minutes. Reduce the heat to low. Tip the pan slightly and use a spoon to scoop out any excess fat, leaving a few tablespoons in the pan. Continue to simmer on low until fully cooked, about 5 more minutes.

MAKES 4 SERVINGS FOR DINNER, OR 8 AS AN APPETIZER
Takes about 50 minutes, plus at least 1 hour for marinating

FOR THE TZATZIKI SAUCE

1½ cups plain Greek yogurt

¼ cup minced cucumber

2 tablespoons chopped fresh flat-leaf parsley

1 clove garlic, peeled and grated

Juice of 1 lemon

¼ teaspoon kosher salt

¼ teaspoon freshly cracked black pepper

FOR THE LAMB

1 pound ground lamb

¼ teaspoon salt

½ teaspoon freshly cracked black pepper

1 small yellow onion, peeled and finely diced

1 clove garlic, peeled and minced

½ teaspoon ground cumin

½ teaspoon dried oregano flakes

¼ teaspoon dried rosemary

2 tablespoons olive oil

1 bag (10 ounces) pita chips
(about 75 chips)

1 cup (4 ounces) shredded
Jack cheese

1 cup (4 ounces) crumbled
feta cheese

1 cup chopped cucumber

1 cup chopped tomato

1 cup chopped kalamata olives
(or your favorite kind)

2 tablespoons olive oil

4 Preheat the broiler to high with a rack about 4 inches from the heat.

5 Arrange the pita chips evenly on a sheet pan, overlapping them as little as possible.

6 Sprinkle the Jack cheese on the chips, distributing it evenly. Next, add the lamb mixture, and finally, top with the feta cheese.

7 Broil until the Jack cheese has melted and the chips are starting to brown, 3 to 5 minutes. (Watch carefully to make sure they don't burn.) Remove from the oven.

8 Top the nachos with the cucumber, tomato, and olives. Remove the tzatziki sauce from the fridge and drizzle it on top. Serve hot.

FALAFEL NACHOS

Falafel—those flavorful Middle Eastern chickpea patties we all know and love—are totally sturdy enough to be nacho chips! You can use store-bought falafel balls for this, which would give them more of a totcho vibe. But I take it a step further and form from-scratch falafel patties that are on the flatter side, like circular chips. In a traditional falafel recipe I wouldn't use flour, but I added a bit to this not-cho version so the falafel "chips" would hold their shape.

*Takes about 1 hour, plus an
overnight soak of the chickpeas*

1½ cups dried chickpeas

1 jalapeño, stemmed
(seeds removed if you
prefer milder heat)

1 clove garlic, peeled

1 teaspoon ground cumin

1 cup chopped fresh flat-leaf
parsley

2 scallions, trimmed and green
and white parts roughly
chopped

¼ cup all-purpose flour

¼ cup olive oil

1 cup (4 ounces) shredded
Jack cheese

1 cup (4 ounces) crumbled
feta cheese

1½ cups hummus

½ cup diced tomato

½ cup diced cucumber

½ cup Herby Crema (page 37)

1 Put the chickpeas in a large bowl and add water to cover. Allow to soak overnight.

2 Drain and rinse the chickpeas. Transfer them to the bowl of a food processor and add the jalapeño, garlic, cumin, parsley, and scallions. Pulse and process until the mixture has the texture of coarse sand.

3 Pour the chickpea mixture into a large bowl and add the flour. Stir to combine.

4 Heat the oil in a large frying pan over medium-high heat.

5 Scoop about ¼ cup of the chickpea mixture into the palm of your hand and press it into a patty, applying enough pressure to help it come together. Gently place it in the hot oil and use a spatula to flatten it. You want it to be about ½ inch thick and 4 inches in diameter. Repeat with more of the chickpea mixture until the pan is full (but not crowded).

6 Working in batches, shape and cook the falafel patties, turning once with a spatula, until they are browned on both sides, about 3 minutes per side. Transfer the patties to a cooling rack or paper towel–lined plate as they cook.

7 When all the falafel patties are done, preheat the broiler to low with a rack about 4 inches from the heat.

8 Arrange the falafel patties evenly on a sheet pan, overlapping them as little as possible. Sprinkle the Jack and feta cheeses on the chips, distributing them evenly.

9 Broil until the Jack cheese has melted and the falafel patties are starting to brown, 3 to 5 minutes. (Watch carefully to make sure they don't burn.) Remove from the oven.

10 Top the falafel chips with the hummus, dolloping it on, and then the tomato and cucumber. Drizzle on the crema and serve hot.

HEARTY COMFORT IN NACHO FORM

CHICKEN PARM NOT-CHOS

With all this chicken-as-the-taco-shell business going on at fast food places, it must have slipped everyone's mind that we could also use the chicken as a chip! So I fixed the problem and made these chicken parm not-chos. They taste amazing and it's not hard for me to eat a ton of them, but there are no real surprises here. It's just chicken parm served a different way. A nacho way. If you don't feel like making your own breaded chicken cutlets, you can use store-bought chicken nuggets or fingers and prepare them according to the package directions (start the recipe at Step 5).

MAKES 2 SERVINGS FOR DINNER, OR 4 AS AN APPETIZER

Takes about 45 minutes

2 boneless, skinless chicken breasts

1 cup all-purpose flour

2 large eggs, beaten

2 cups seasoned bread crumbs

1 cup grated Parmesan cheese

Kosher salt and freshly cracked black pepper

Vegetable or peanut oil

½ cup tomato sauce

1 cup (4 ounces) shredded low-moisture mozzarella cheese

Minced fresh flat-leaf parsley, for garnish

Crushed red pepper flakes, for garnish

1 Place a chicken breast on your work surface and put the palm of your hand on top of it. Carefully run your knife through the chicken breast, slicing it the long way into 2 or 3 thinner pieces. Cover with parchment paper and use a kitchen mallet or small skillet to pound the chicken to about ¼-inch thickness. Remove the parchment paper and cut the chicken into chip-size triangles. Repeat with the other one. You should have about 25 triangles.

2 Place the flour in a bowl, the eggs in another, and mix the bread crumbs and Parmesan cheese in a third. Season each bowl with a pinch of salt and pepper.

3 Bread the chicken triangles by dipping them in the flour first, then the egg, then coating with the bread crumb and cheese mixture.

4 Pour oil into a heavy-bottomed frying pan to a depth of ½ inch. Heat over medium-high heat. Add the chicken "chips" to the hot oil, about 5 at a time depending on the size of your frying pan (you don't want to crowd them). Cook, turning once, until browned on both sides, about 4 minutes. Transfer to a cooling rack or paper towel–lined plate.

5 Preheat the broiler to low with a rack about 4 inches from the heat.

6 Arrange the chicken chips on a sheet pan, overlapping them as little as possible. Top the chips first with a drizzle of the sauce, then the mozzarella cheese.

7 Broil until the cheese is starting to brown, about 5 minutes. (Watch carefully to make sure they don't burn.) Remove from the oven.

8 Garnish the nachos with the parsley and red pepper flakes. Serve hot.

CHICKEN BROCCOLI ALFREDO NACHOS

Nothing screams "family dinner" to me like chicken broccoli ziti. It was a staple in my house growing up and one of the few ways my mom could get us to eat a vegetable. Considering that I'm making a case for nachos for dinner, it seemed obvious I had to nachofy this dish. I thought a creamy Alfredo sauce, instead of the regular cheese topping, would help tie the classic pasta dish to the nachos. I like my broccoli charred, so I broil it first on its own, then put it on top of the chips and broil it again.

1 Place the chicken pieces on a plate and rub with the salt, pepper, paprika, and Italian seasoning.

2 Heat 1 tablespoon of the oil in a large frying pan over medium-high heat. Add the chicken pieces and cook for about 7 minutes. Flip and cook for another 5 minutes, or until cooked through. Remove from the heat and transfer the chicken to a cutting board to cool for 5 minutes.

3 Chop the chicken into ¾-inch cubes.

4 Preheat the broiler to low with a rack about 4 inches from the heat.

5 Spread the broccoli on a sheet pan and drizzle the remaining tablespoon of oil on top. Toss with your hands to coat and season with a pinch of salt. Broil until lightly charred, 3 to 5 minutes. (Watch carefully to make sure it doesn't burn.) Remove from the oven and transfer the broccoli to a large bowl. Wipe the sheet pan clean.

6 Meanwhile, make the Alfredo sauce: Melt the butter in a small pot over medium heat. Add the garlic and cook, stirring, until fragrant, about 2 minutes. Add the cream and bring to a simmer. Remove from the heat and add the Parmesan. Stir well to allow the cheese to melt.

7 Arrange the tortilla chips evenly on the cleaned sheet pan, overlapping them as little as possible.

8 Sprinkle the mozzarella cheese on the chips, distributing it evenly. Top with the chicken, then drizzle on the Alfredo sauce. Finally, top with the broccoli.

9 Broil until the chips and sauce are starting to brown, 3 to 5 minutes. (Again, watch carefully to make sure they don't burn.) Remove from the oven and serve hot.

MAKES 4 SERVINGS
FOR DINNER, OR
8 AS AN APPETIZER
Takes about 40 minutes

1 pound boneless, skinless chicken breasts, sliced in half the flat way to make them thinner

¼ teaspoon kosher salt, plus extra as needed

¼ teaspoon freshly cracked black pepper

1 teaspoon smoked paprika

1 teaspoon dried Italian seasoning

2 tablespoons olive oil

1 cup chopped broccoli

4 tablespoons (½ stick) unsalted butter

1 clove garlic, peeled and minced

¾ cup heavy cream

1 cup freshly grated Parmesan cheese

1 bag (12 ounces) tortilla chips (about 90 chips)

1 cup (4 ounces) shredded low-moisture mozzarella cheese

CHICKEN TIKKA MASALA NAANCHOS

**MAKES 4 SERVINGS
FOR DINNER, OR
8 AS AN APPETIZER**

Takes about 55 minutes

**FOR THE CHICKEN TIKKA
MASALA**

2 tablespoons unsalted butter

1 jalapeño, stemmed
(seeds removed if you prefer
milder heat) and diced

1 small white onion, peeled and
diced

1 pound boneless, skinless
chicken breast, cut into 1-inch
pieces

1 teaspoon kosher salt

1 tablespoon grated garlic

1 tablespoon grated ginger

1 can (14 ounces) crushed
tomatoes

½ cup coconut milk

1 tablespoon garam masala

Whenever I eat Indian food, I use naan as a scoop for the other foods—kind of like nacho chips! Which got me thinking about what would happen if I nachofied chicken tikka masala, another famous mash-up dish (its specific origins are debated but seem undoubtedly linked to Britain's colonization of India). Here I take the dish farther into nacho territory by crisping up the naan, layering the chicken tikka masala on top, and adding some cheese and chutney as a topping. These nachos are bursting with flavors! The cilantro chutney brightens up the rich, saucy chicken and would taste awesome on so many different nachos.

1 Make the chicken tikka masala: Melt the butter in a large frying pan over medium-high heat. Add the jalapeño and onion and stir to combine. Cook, stirring occasionally, until softened, about 5 minutes.

2 Add the chicken and season with the salt. Cook, stirring occasionally, until the chicken is starting to brown, about 5 minutes. Add the garlic and ginger and cook, stirring, until they are fragrant and golden, about 2 minutes.

3 Stir in the tomatoes, coconut milk, and garam masala. Bring to a simmer, then reduce the heat to low. Simmer, uncovered, until the sauce thickens slightly and the chicken is fully cooked and tender, about 15 minutes.

FOR THE CILANTRO
CHUTNEY

2 cups fresh cilantro, plus extra
for garnish

1 tablespoon olive oil

1 clove garlic, peeled and
grated

1 jalapeño, stemmed
(seeds removed if you
prefer milder heat)

Juice of 1 lime

1 teaspoon grated ginger

¼ teaspoon kosher salt

FOR THE NACHOS

6 rounds (24 ounces) naan
bread, each cut into 6 to 8
triangles

3 cups (12 ounces) shredded
Jack cheese

4 Meanwhile, make the cilantro chutney: Combine the
cilantro, olive oil, garlic, jalapeño, lime juice, ginger,
and salt in a blender. Blend until smooth. Set aside.

5 Make the nachos: Preheat the oven to 400°F with a rack
in the center of the oven.

6 Spread the naan triangles on sheet pans (you may need
to do this in a couple of batches depending on how many
pans you have). Bake until they start to brown and get
crispy, about 10 minutes.

7 Turn the broiler to low.

8 Transfer all the naan onto a sheet pan. Top with half of
the cheese.

9 Spoon the chicken mixture evenly over the chips. Top with
the remaining cheese.

10 Broil for 3 to 5 minutes, until the cheese is melted.
(Watch carefully to make sure the nachos don't burn.)
Remove from the oven.

11 Top the nachos with the chutney and garnish with chopped
cilantro. Serve hot.

BBQ PULLED PORK NACHOS

When I was thinking about how to set this plate of nachos apart from other nachos topped with bland pulled pork, I was inspired by BBQ pizza, which is usually topped with red onion and fresh parsley. I also added creamy coleslaw, as I would on a pulled pork sandwich, to help balance the heavy flavors with something bright and fresh. For the pork, start with the carnitas recipe and then add some BBQ sauce for that Tex-Mex BBQ magic.

1 Put the carnitas in a small microwave-safe bowl and stir in the BBQ sauce. Microwave for 1 minute on high to warm.

2 Preheat the broiler to low with a rack about 4 inches from the heat.

3 Arrange the tortilla chips evenly on a sheet pan, overlapping them as little as possible.

4 Sprinkle the cheddar cheese on the chips, distributing it evenly. Next top with the carnitas and onion. Finally, top with the Jack cheese.

5 Broil until the cheese has melted and the chips are starting to brown, 3 to 5 minutes. (Watch carefully to make sure they don't burn.) Remove from the oven.

6 Top the nachos with the slaw and cilantro. Serve hot.

MAKES 4 SERVINGS FOR DINNER, OR 8 AS AN APPETIZER

Takes about 20 minutes

1½ cups carnitas (preferably homemade; see page 50)

¼ cup your favorite BBQ sauce

1 bag (12 ounces) tortilla chips (about 90 chips)

2 cups (8 ounces) shredded cheddar cheese

¼ cup thinly sliced red onion

1 cup (4 ounces) shredded Jack cheese

2 cups Creamy Crunchy Slaw (page 26)

¼ cup chopped fresh cilantro

LASAGN'CHOS

**MAKES 4 SERVINGS
FOR DINNER, OR
8 AS AN APPETIZER**

Takes about 90 minutes

1 pound ground beef
(90% lean)

1 small white onion, peeled
and diced

Kosher salt

3 cloves garlic, peeled and
minced

1 can (28 ounces) crushed
tomatoes

1 tablespoon dried oregano
flakes

1 teaspoon crushed red pepper
flakes

2 tablespoons heavy cream

½ cup grated Parmesan cheese

1 pound dried lasagna noodles

Vegetable or peanut oil,
for frying

1 cup (4 ounces) shredded low-
moisture mozzarella cheese

2 cups (about 16 ounces) ricotta
cheese

¼ cup chopped fresh flat-leaf
parsley

It's crazy how well fried pasta works as nacho chips. I was experimenting with turning pasta into chips and tried cutting lasagna sheets into triangles to give them a proper nacho look. After I successfully made the pasta chips, I decided it made sense to go all-in on lasagna. I made a meaty bolognese sauce and layered it on the lasagna chips with mozzarella, ricotta, and parm. These nachos started as a crazy idea—but the final result works way better than I ever imagined. This recipe is a little bit involved, but it's entirely worth it; to save yourself some time, put the pasta water on to boil while the tomato sauce is simmering in Step 2.

1 Combine the beef and onion in a medium-size saucepan over high heat. Season with salt. Cook, stirring often, to brown the meat, about 8 minutes. Drain any excess fat from the pan, then add the garlic and cook, stirring occasionally, until it is fragrant and turning golden, about 2 minutes.

2 Add the tomatoes, oregano, and red pepper flakes and bring to a simmer. Reduce the heat to low and simmer, uncovered, about 30 minutes. Add the cream and 1/4 cup of the Parmesan, stirring to combine. Cover and let simmer until ready to use.

3 While the sauce simmers, generously season a large pot of water with salt and bring it to a boil over high heat.

4 Drop the pasta into the water, stirring to separate the sheets, and cook until just shy of al dente (it should still be slightly crunchy), about 7 minutes.

5 Drain the pasta in a strainer and drizzle a little oil in the strainer to prevent it from sticking.

6 Place a lasagna sheet on a cutting board and cut it crosswise into 3 rectangles, then slice each rectangle in half diagonally to form triangles. Repeat with the remaining lasagna sheets.

7 Pour oil into a large frying pan to a depth of about 1 inch and heat over medium heat. Add the pasta in batches, being careful not to overcrowd the pan, and fry until browned on the bottom, about 2 minutes. Flip with tongs and cook on the second side until browned, about 1 minute. Transfer to a cooling rack or paper towel–lined plate. Repeat with the remaining pasta until all the "chips" are cooked.

8 Preheat the broiler to low with a rack about 4 inches from the heat.

9 Arrange the chips evenly on a sheet pan, overlapping them as little as possible. Sprinkle on the mozzarella cheese, distributing it evenly. Drizzle on the sauce, then add dollops of the ricotta cheese. Top with the remaining parm.

10 Broil until the mozzarella has melted, 3 to 5 minutes. (Watch carefully to make sure the nachos don't burn.) Remove from the oven.

11 Top the nachos with the parsley. Serve hot.

BEEF BULGOGI NACHOS

**MAKES 4 SERVINGS
FOR DINNER, OR
8 AS AN APPETIZER**

*Takes about 30 minutes, plus at
least 30 minutes for marinating*

FOR THE BULGOGI BEEF

1 pound sirloin tips, thinly
sliced against the grain,
about ¼ inch thick

1 tablespoon gochujang
(Korean red chili paste)

1 pear, cored and grated

¼ cup toasted sesame oil

¼ cup rice vinegar

2 tablespoons sesame seeds

1 tablespoon gochugaru
(Korean chili flakes)

2 tablespoons honey

2 tablespoons soy sauce

1 tablespoon vegetable oil

Korean–Tex-Mex mash-ups are pretty common, and for good reason: The flavors meld together well. The tortilla chips and Jack cheese used here represent the Tex-Mex flavors, while the bulgogi beef and kimchi offer some Korean inspiration. Bulgogi translates to "fire meat" in English—an apt description of the chargrilled slices of tender marinated meat (often but not always beef). My take features a salty-sweet marinade (the interplay of those flavors is a hallmark of the dish) and beef seared in a hot frying pan. The results are super flavorful, and when combined with the creamy, melty cheese and little pops of edamame, make for awesome nachos. A fresh cucumber salsa rounds it all out.

1 Make the bulgogi beef: Put the beef in a large bowl and add the gochujang, grated pear, sesame oil, rice vinegar, sesame seeds, gochugaru, honey, and soy sauce. Stir to combine and coat. Cover and allow to marinate for at least 30 minutes at room temperature or overnight in the fridge.

2 When ready to cook, heat the vegetable oil in a large frying pan over medium-high heat. Add the beef and its marinade and cook on high, stirring often, until the beef is cooked through and crispy at the edges, 5 to 7 minutes. Transfer the beef to a cutting board to cool.

3 Make the salsa: Combine the cucumber, tomato, onion, garlic, jalapeños, cilantro, vinegar, and salt in a medium-size bowl and stir well. Adjust the salt, garlic, and vinegar to taste. Set aside.

4 Make the nachos: Preheat the broiler to high with a rack about 4 inches from the heat.

5 Arrange the tortilla chips evenly on a sheet pan, overlapping them as little as possible.

6 Top the chips with half of the cheese, distributing it evenly. Add the bulgogi beef, then the kimchi, and then the remaining cheese.

7 Broil until the cheese has melted and the chips are starting to brown, 3 to 5 minutes. (Watch carefully to make sure they don't burn.) Remove from the oven.

8 Top the nachos with the edamame and cucumber salsa or serve the salsa on the side if desired. Serve hot.

FOR THE SALSA

1 English cucumber, diced

1 tomato, stemmed and diced

½ large white onion, peeled and diced

½ clove garlic, peeled and minced, plus extra as needed

2 jalapeños, stemmed (seeds removed if you prefer milder heat) and diced

2 tablespoons chopped fresh cilantro

1 tablespoon rice vinegar, plus extra as needed

¼ teaspoon kosher salt, plus extra as needed

FOR THE NACHOS

1 bag (12 ounces) tortilla chips (about 90 chips)

2 cups (8 ounces) shredded Jack cheese

1 cup chopped kimchi

½ cup cooked edamame

STROGANACHOS

**MAKES 4 SERVINGS
FOR DINNER, OR
8 AS AN APPETIZER**

Takes about 35 minutes

2 tablespoons unsalted butter

1 pound "stir-fry" steak
(sirloin or a similar cut,
cut into 1-inch cubes)

4 ounces baby bella
mushrooms, trimmed and
sliced

1 cup sour cream

1 bag (12 ounces) tortilla chips
(about 90 chips)

2 cups (8 ounces) shredded
Jack cheese

¼ cup chopped fresh flat-leaf
parsley

¼ cup sliced cornichons

½ cup Lime Crema (page 35)

Beef stroganoff was one of my favorite meals when I was growing up. I think my mom realized she could serve the family beef and sour cream (two of our favorite things) under the guise of being worldly, and it was an all-around win. When I was figuring out which family dinners to nachofy, stroganoff was an obvious choice—and you know it's going to be a winner when the name itself blends seamlessly with the word "nachos." Plus, sour cream is at home on nachos, so it makes sense!

1 Melt the butter in a large frying pan over medium-high heat. Add the steak and cook, stirring occasionally, until browned on the edges, about 4 minutes.

2 Add the mushrooms and cook, stirring occasionally, until the mushrooms and steak have browned and the steak is medium-well done, about 5 minutes. Remove from the heat and add the sour cream. Stir well to combine.

3 Preheat the broiler to high with a rack about 4 inches from the heat.

4 Arrange the tortilla chips evenly on a sheet pan, overlapping them as little as possible.

5 Sprinkle 1 cup of the cheese on the chips, distributing it evenly. Next add the steak mixture, then top with the remaining 1 cup of cheese.

6 Broil until the cheese has melted and the chips are starting to brown, 3 to 5 minutes. (Watch carefully to make sure they don't burn.) Remove from the oven.

7 Top the nachos with the parsley, cornichons, and crema. Serve hot.

SHRIMP AND GRITS NACHOS

Grits, a New World food that originated with the Indigenous Muscogee in the sixteenth century, are made with stone-ground corn, which gives them the gritty texture they are known and named for. Hugely popular in the South, first among the Gullah Geechee, descendants of West African slaves, who were given small amounts of cornmeal as a food allowance, grits eventually became a common dish among laborers and fishermen, and that's where the addition of seafood really took off.

My first experience with fish and grits was through a song by Outkast—my favorite music group of all time. I eventually encountered true grits thanks to my then girlfriend, now wife, Georgina, who grew up in Georgia and whose mother makes the best grits ever. For years I tried and failed to make proper grits; it was not until I bought *Jubilee* by Toni Tipton-Martin that I finally started making grits that were up to Georgina's standards!

When prepared properly—as Toni Tipton-Martin's book taught me—cornmeal grits can be smooth and creamy like a cheese sauce. From cheese sauce, it's a natural leap to nachos! I decided to drizzle creamy grits over tortilla chips, then top them with andouille sausage and chopped shrimp, making sure there were plenty of pan juices and extra hot sauce to go around. The first time I made this recipe I didn't think it would work, but boy was I wrong. All the flavors of shrimp and grits served up on a chip!

1 Combine the stock and milk in a medium-size saucepan and bring to a simmer over medium-low heat. Whisk in the cornmeal, then add the salt. Bring back to a simmer, then reduce the heat to low. Cook, whisking often, until the grits are tender and have fully come together, about 20 minutes.

2 Remove the grits from the heat and stir in the cheese and butter. Add a splash of milk or stock if the mixture appears to be too thick.

3 Meanwhile, cook the sausage in a large frying pan over medium-high heat until it is browned on the edges and some of the fat has rendered, about 3 minutes. Add the shrimp and cook, stirring and tossing, until the shrimp are cooked through, about 3 minutes. Remove from the heat.

4 Preheat the broiler to low with a rack about 4 inches from the heat.

5 Arrange the tortilla chips evenly on a sheet pan, overlapping them as little as possible.

6 Stir the grits and pour them on top of the chips, distributing them evenly. Next add the sausage and then the shrimp.

7 Broil until everything is heated through and the chips start browning at the edges, 3 to 5 minutes. (Watch carefully to make sure they don't burn.) Remove from the oven.

8 Top the nachos with the parsley and serve hot.

MAKES 4 SERVINGS FOR DINNER, OR 8 AS AN APPETIZER
Takes about 50 minutes

2 cups chicken stock, plus extra as needed

2 cups milk, plus extra as needed

¾ cup stone-ground cornmeal (medium grind, not instant grits)

½ tablespoon kosher salt

1½ cups (6 ounces) shredded cheddar cheese

2 tablespoons unsalted butter

½ pound andouille sausage, cut into quarter-rounds

½ pound shrimp, peeled, deveined, and each cut into 3 or 4 pieces

1 bag (12 ounces) tortilla chips (about 90 chips)

¼ cup chopped fresh flat-leaf parsley

SPICY 5-PEPPER NACHOS

**MAKES 4 SERVINGS
FOR DINNER, OR
8 AS AN APPETIZER**

Takes about 20 minutes

1 cucumber, diced

5 red Thai chilis, stemmed
(seeds removed if you prefer
milder heat) and minced

1 scallion, trimmed and green
and white parts sliced

1 clove garlic, peeled and
grated

2 tablespoons chopped fresh
cilantro

2 teaspoons honey

Kosher salt and freshly cracked
black pepper

2 poblano peppers

1 bag (12 ounces) tortilla chips
(about 90 chips)

1 canned chipotle chile in
adobo, chopped, plus
1 tablespoon adobo sauce
from the can

1 batch Nacho Cheese Sauce
(page 7)

1 cup Spicy Habanero Carnitas
(page 51)

About 20 pickled pepper slices
(store-bought or homemade;
see page 29)

Spicy food is the best, and nachos are a great place to bring the heat. I wanted to make a nacho that had five different toppings, with the flavor of a different type of pepper infused into each. I put habanero in the pork, chipotle in the cheese, and Thai chilis in the salsa, and I topped the whole thing with roasted poblanos and pickled Fresnos. I decided to use cucumbers as the base of the salsa to provide a slight respite from the heat, but cucumbers won't save you, my friends. This is one of my favorite recipes in the whole book, but proceed with caution!

1 Stir together the cucumber, Thai chilis, scallion, garlic, cilantro, and honey in a small bowl. Season to taste with salt and pepper. Set aside.

2 Preheat the broiler to high with a rack about 4 inches from the heat.

3 Line a small baking sheet with the aluminum foil and arrange the poblanos on top. Broil the poblanos, turning occasionally, until fully charred black, about 4 minutes per side. Remove from the oven. Transfer to a small bowl and cover tightly with plastic wrap. Allow to sit for 10 minutes.

4 Turn the broiler to low.

5 Arrange the tortilla chips evenly on a sheet pan, overlapping them as little as possible.

6 Stir the chipotle and adobo sauce into the cheese sauce.

7 Uncover the poblanos and use a paring knife (and your fingers) to peel off the charred skin and remove the seeds. Slice the peppers into thin 1-inch-long slices.

8 Drizzle half of the cheese sauce onto the chips, distributing it evenly. Top with the carnitas and poblanos, then drizzle on the remaining cheese sauce.

9 Broil until everything is warmed through and the chips are starting to brown, 3 to 5 minutes. (Watch carefully to make sure they don't burn.) Remove from the oven.

10 Top the nachos with the salsa and pickled Fresnos. Serve hot.

PIEROGI NACHOS

Yes, pierogi can be chips, too! They are commonly served with sour cream for dipping, so in my mind, they basically already *are* chips. I topped these nachofied pierogis with melty cheddar cheese and chives, as well as the Power Crema from page 36, but feel free to add caramelized onions, crumbled bacon and/or cooked kielbasa, or even sauerkraut. (You can also swap in your favorite kind of pierogi if you don't want to use potato pierogi.)

1 Preheat the broiler to low with a rack about 4 inches from the heat.

2 Arrange the pierogi on a sheet pan so they are in a single layer with some overlapping, not spread apart on the pan. Sprinkle the cheese on top, distributing it evenly.

3 Broil until the cheese has melted and the pierogis are starting to brown, 3 to 5 minutes. (Watch carefully to make sure they don't burn.) Remove from the oven.

4 Top the nachos with the crema and chives. Serve hot.

MAKES 4 SERVINGS FOR DINNER, OR 8 AS AN APPETIZER
Takes about 15 minutes

1 package (32 ounces) frozen potato pierogi, baked according to package directions

2 cups (8 ounces) shredded cheddar cheese

½ cup Power Crema

¼ cup chopped fresh chives

PRETZEL BRATCHOS

**MAKES 4 SERVINGS
FOR DINNER, OR
8 AS AN APPETIZER**

Takes about 35 minutes

24 ounces soft pretzel
nuggets

3 bratwurst (about 1¼ pounds
total), cooked and sliced into
rounds

¼ cup pilsner beer

1 teaspoon crushed red pepper
flakes

1 batch Nacho Cheese Sauce
(page 7)

1½ cups sauerkraut, drained

think this should be on the menu at every beer hall and bier-
garten. What's not to like? Big chewy soft pretzels, salty
bratwurst, and tangy sauerkraut, all smothered in a spicy beer
cheese. If you can't find soft pretzel nuggets near you (I usually
buy them at the fresh breads section at Whole Foods), use bigger
soft pretzels and cut them into 2-inch pieces. You could also use
sliced soft pretzel buns.

1 Preheat the oven to 350°F with a rack in the center.

2 Arrange the pretzel nuggets evenly on a sheet pan,
overlapping them as little as possible. Top evenly with
the bratwurst.

3 Bake the pretzels and brats until warmed through, about
10 minutes.

4 Meanwhile, stir the beer and red pepper flakes into the
cheese sauce. If needed, microwave the sauce in 15-second
increments until it is warm and easily pourable.

5 Remove the pretzels and brats from the oven and pour
the cheese sauce over them. Top with the sauerkraut and
serve hot.

MUSHROOM TOFU NACHOS

This recipe is inspired by the Sichuan dish mapo tofu, which is easily one of my favorite comfort foods when I am feeling under the weather. Instead of using meat in these nachos, as is common in that dish, I went with a vegetarian mushroom version. If you have ever had mapo tofu, you know it has deep, deep umami flavors and lots of tongue-numbing spice (thanks to Sichuan peppercorns). These nachos definitely deliver on those promises. Can you tell I like the spicy ones?

MAKES 4 SERVINGS
FOR DINNER, OR
8 AS AN APPETIZER
Takes about 45 minutes

1 tablespoon chili oil

1 teaspoon ground
Sichuan peppercorns
(see Note, page 132)

16 ounces baby bella
mushrooms, sliced

1 teaspoon grated garlic

1 teaspoon grated ginger

2 tablespoons spicy fermented
broad bean paste
(see Note, page 132)

1 tablespoon soy sauce

1 tablespoon Shaoxing cooking
wine (see Note, page 132)

1 block (14 ounces) medium-
firm tofu, drained and sliced
into ¾-inch cubes

1 bag (12 ounces) tortilla chips
(about 90 chips)

2 cups (8 ounces) shredded
Jack cheese

¼ cup pickled jalapeño or
Fresno slices (store-bought
or homemade; see page 29)

¼ cup chopped fresh cilantro

1 Combine the chili oil, Sichuan peppercorns, and mushrooms in a large frying pan over medium-high heat. Cook, stirring often, until the mushrooms have reduced in size and browned, about 4 minutes.

2 Add the garlic and ginger and cook until fragrant and golden, about 2 minutes. Add the bean paste, soy sauce, and Shaoxing wine and stir to combine. Add the tofu and stir to coat. Bring to a simmer, then reduce the heat to low. Simmer until the flavors meld and the tofu is heated through, about 15 minutes. Remove from the heat.

3 Preheat the broiler to low with a rack about 4 inches from the heat.

4 Arrange the tortilla chips evenly on a sheet pan, overlapping them as little as possible.

5 Sprinkle half of the cheese on the chips, distributing it evenly. Spoon the tofu mixture over the chips, then top with the remaining cheese.

6 Broil until the cheese has melted and the chips are beginning to brown, 3 to 5 minutes. (Watch carefully to make sure they don't burn.) Remove from the oven.

7 Top the nachos with the pickled peppers and cilantro. Serve hot.

NOTE: Sichuan peppercorns are a mouth-tingling spice that, because of their numbing properties, make it easier to enjoy the flavors of hot foods like chilies. Spicy fermented broad bean paste is a deeply flavored paste that adds the super-savory umami notes to this dish, and Shaoxing cooking wine is a mildly flavored rice wine that is common in many Chinese recipes (I always have some on hand because so many call for it). I usually buy these ingredients at a Chinese market near me, but they are available online as well.

BRUNCH AND MIDNIGHT SNACK'CHOS

CHILAQUILES

MAKES 4 SERVINGS FOR DINNER OR BRUNCH, OR 8 AS AN APPETIZER

Takes about 50 minutes

1½ cups Green Tomatillo Salsa (page 23) or Roasted Tomato Salsa (page 22)

1 batch Tortilla Chips (page 4), or 1 bag (12 ounces) sturdy artisanal tortilla chips, such as Mi Niña

2 tablespoons unsalted butter

4 large eggs

1 cup (4 ounces) crumbled Cotija cheese

½ cup chopped fresh cilantro

1 cup Power Crema (page 36)

I love chilaquiles so much, I order them anytime I see them on a menu. While chilaquiles and nachos share some similarities (Fried tortilla chips? Check. Chiles? Check.), chilaquiles are often eaten for breakfast in Mexico, and they are typically saucier than nachos. So is it cheating to put chilaquiles in a nachos cookbook? Well . . . not when we're having chilaquiles for breakfast and nachos for dinner! This is the only recipe in the book where I strongly urge you to make your own chips—or at the very least use an artisanal brand that tastes homemade (but really, you should make your own if you can!). Sturdy chips are essential in chilaquiles because you want the chips to stay crisp in the sauce; industrial-style chips will become a soggy mess.

1 Pour the salsa into a large frying pan and bring to a simmer over medium heat.

2 Working in batches, add the chips to the pan and toss to coat. Cook, stirring, until the sauce clings to the chips, about 3 minutes. Transfer to a sheet pan and spread into an even layer.

3 Meanwhile, melt the butter in another large frying pan over high heat. Crack the eggs into the pan and reduce the heat to medium. Cook sunny-side up until the egg whites are set, 3 to 5 minutes.

4 Top the sauced chips with the cheese, distributing it evenly. Add the fried eggs, then the cilantro, and finally the crema. Serve hot.

BREAKFAST NACHOS

Chilaquiles is a more traditional version of nachos in breakfast form, but I wanted to try a riff that is straight-up bacon and eggs on chips. These would be a big hit at a fancy brunch place—just don't forget the Bloody Marys and mimosas!

1 Melt the butter in a large frying pan over medium heat.

2 Beat the eggs with a fork until fully smooth. Pour the egg mixture into the frying pan and continue to stir constantly with a spatula as you cook gently, lowering the heat if needed.

3 Cook until the eggs are just starting to set up, but continue to whisk so the curds are small and soft. Just when they look like they are about done, remove from the heat and stir in the sour cream.

4 Preheat the broiler to low with a rack about 4 inches from the heat.

5 Arrange the tortilla chips evenly on a sheet pan, overlapping them as little as possible.

6 Top the chips with the pepper Jack cheese. Next top with the bacon and sausage, and then the cheddar cheese.

7 Broil on high for 3 to 5 minutes, until the cheese is melted and the chips are starting to brown. (Watch carefully to make sure they don't burn.) Remove from the oven.

8 Top the nachos evenly with the soft scrambled eggs. Add with the salsa, crema, and hot sauce (or serve them on the side). Serve hot.

MAKES 4 SERVINGS FOR DINNER, OR 8 AS AN APPETIZER
Takes about 35 minutes

2 tablespoons unsalted butter

6 large eggs

¼ cup sour cream

1 bag (12 ounces) tortilla chips (about 90 chips)

1 cup (4 ounces) shredded pepper Jack cheese

5 slices bacon, cooked and crumbled

5 links cooked sausage, sliced into rounds

1½ cups (6 ounces) shredded cheddar cheese

1 cup Roasted Tomato Salsa (page 22)

½ cup Lime Crema (page 35)

½ cup chipotle sauce (store-bought or homemade; see page 21)

CHICKEN AND WAFFLE NACHOS

When I was first developing this recipe, I wanted to put the chicken *on* the waffles, but it wasn't really working out. Once I realized that the chicken serves as a chip in its own way, it all came together for me. I use frozen chicken strips and waffles for this and have zero shame about it—it makes these nachos pretty effortless. Besides, most waffle irons make waffles that are too thick to serve as chips, and the frozen kind just work so perfectly. That said, if you want to try making these with your favorite homemade waffles and chicken tenders, be my guest (and let me know how it turns out)!

MAKES 4 SERVINGS FOR DINNER, OR 8 AS AN APPETIZER

Takes about 55 minutes

1 bag (25 ounces) frozen breaded chicken strips

20 frozen waffles, halved

1 cup (4 ounces) shredded cheddar cheese

1 cup (4 ounces) shredded Jack cheese

About 20 pickled jalapeño slices (store-bought or homemade; see page 29)

2 scallions, trimmed and green and white parts sliced

½ cup maple syrup

¼ cup hot sauce

1 Cook the chicken according to the package directions (breaking up any large pieces so the pieces are all about the same size).

2 Meanwhile, cook the waffles according to the package directions, adding 1 to 2 minutes to the cooking time so they get crunchy.

3 Preheat the oven to 500°F with a rack in the center.

4 Arrange the waffles in an even layer on a sheet pan, overlapping them as little as possible. Top with the chicken, distributing it evenly, then add the cheddar and Jack cheeses and jalapeño slices.

5 Bake until the cheeses have melted, about 5 minutes. Remove from the oven.

6 Top the nachos with the scallions, syrup, and hot sauce. Serve hot.

BISCUIT AND GRAVY NACHOS

MAKES 4 SERVINGS
FOR DINNER, OR
8 AS AN APPETIZER

Takes about 40 minutes

2 tubes (16.3 ounces each)
   refrigerated biscuits
   (any style works)

½ pound bulk breakfast
   sausage

1 small onion, peeled and
   diced

2 tablespoons unsalted butter

¼ cup all-purpose flour

4 cups milk

Kosher salt and freshly cracked
   black pepper

2 cups (8 ounces) shredded
   cheddar cheese

¼ cup chopped fresh flat-leaf
   parsley

Biscuits and gravy are the dark horse of brunch—they always sit there on the menu, unassuming and easily overlooked, but amazing when you finally decide to order them. I normally love homemade biscuits, but for these nachos, the canned, refrigerated kind really work best. They flake right in half and won't crumble under the weight of the toppings like homemade ones will.

1 Bake the biscuits according to the package directions. Remove from the oven and let cool.

2 Meanwhile, place the sausage in a large frying pan over medium-high heat and cook, stirring and breaking up the meat, until slightly browned and some fat has rendered, about 5 minutes. Add the onion and continue to cook, stirring occasionally, until lightly browned, about 10 minutes.

3 Add the butter to the pan with the sausage and onion, turn the heat down to medium, and let the butter melt. Add the flour and cook, stirring, until the flour and butter have come together to form a roux (the mixture should have the texture of a thin paste), about 3 minutes. Add the milk and stir well to combine. Season to taste with salt and pepper and continue to cook until the mixture comes to a simmer and thickens up, about 5 minutes. Reduce the heat to low and keep warm until ready to use.

4 Turn the oven to 450°F with one rack in the center of the oven and another 4 inches from the heat.

5 Open the cooled biscuits by grabbing the top and bottom and gently prying them apart (most store-bought biscuits have many layers, making this easy to do). Cut the biscuits into semicircles and arrange them on a sheet pan (it's okay if they overlap a bit). Bake on the center rack until they're crisped up a little, about 8 minutes. Remove from the oven.

6 Turn the oven to broil on low.

7 Rearrange the biscuits so that areas that might have been overlapping are now uncovered. Sprinkle half of the cheese on top of the biscuits, distributing it evenly, then drizzle the gravy evenly over all the biscuits. Top with the remaining cheese.

8 Broil on the upper rack until the cheese has melted and some of the biscuits and cheese are starting to brown, 3 to 5 minutes. (Watch carefully to make sure they don't burn.) Remove from the oven.

9 Top the nachos with the parsley. Serve hot.

TRASHY MICROWAVE NACHOS

MAKES 1 SERVING

Takes about 5 minutes

About 15 tortilla chips

½ cup (2 ounces) shredded cheddar cheese

10 pickled jalapeño slices (store-bought or homemade; see page 29)

1 jar (15.5 ounces) salsa, for dumping or dipping

I already talked about my love of microwave nachos on page vi, but they definitely deserve their own recipe. The real magic of microwave nachos that you don't really get in the oven-baked counterpart is the bubbled dried-out bits of cheese. When I was growing up, my family had a rule that if you ever made a plate of these, you had to make a "public announcement" to anyone in the house that nachos were available. Everyone would drop what they were doing and run to the kitchen.

1 Arrange the chips evenly on a microwave-safe plate, overlapping them as little as possible. Sprinkle the cheese on top of the chips, distributing it evenly. Top with the jalapeño slices.

2 Microwave on high for about 45 seconds, until the cheese has melted (bonus points if the edge of the plate is spackled with bubbled, crispy cheese).

3 Dump the salsa on top, or just open the jar and dip the nachos into it one by one. Serve hot.

Xtra Trashy Options

• Make them with Cool Ranch Doritos. Or Fritos. Or Bugles.

• Put Cheez Whiz on top.

• Dump a jar of queso on there.

• Or how about American cheese singles?

• Two words: HOT DOGS.

• Use cheesy puffs instead of chips for cheese-on-cheese action.

• Use spicy chips and pepper Jack cheese, top with sriracha, and feel the burn.

NACHOFY ANYTHING!

Nachos are just a state of mind, man. The key to most alt-chip nacho recipes is keeping the toppings classic nacho. Think carne asada fries, totchos, and other piles of food that are topped with cheese and whatever else you crave.

For the base, start with one of the following (enough to fill a half-sheet pan), cooked:

- French fries
- tater tots
- gnocchi
- mozzarella sticks
- egg rolls
- chicken nuggets
- pizza rolls
- bagel bites
- spanakopita

Top them with the following and broil on low until the cheese melts and the "chips" start to brown, 3 to 5 minutes:

- 2 cups shredded cheese (a mix of cheddar and Jack is traditional, but you can also switch up the cheeses to complement whatever you are using as chips)
- 1 cup taco meat (or carne asada in the case of the fries)
- ½ cup pickled jalapeños slices

Finally, top the not-chos with any or all of the following:

- Pico de Gallo (page 14) or another salsa (see pages 15 to 23)
- Power Crema (page 36) or another crema (see pages 35 to 37)
- Guacamole (page 31) or another gua-ption (see pages 32 to 33)

And that is how you make _____ chos!

- These are also great with whatever leftovers you have around. I have a running segment on my Instagram Story (@tfimb) where I post my Microwave Nachos of the Day (M.N.O.T.D). I usually just top them with the meal I made the day before.

- One final thought: There's no shame in Nacholand. I have definitely poured the crumbs from the bottom of a chip bag into a jar of salsa and eaten it with a spoon. Just saying . . .

Strawberry Shortcake Nachos

Brownies à la Mode 'Chos

Apple Pie Nachos

Sweet 'n' Salty Nachos

Churrochos

Nacho Inspo for Dessert!

Raspberry Cheesecake Nachos

S'mores Nachos

APPLE PIE NACHOS

**MAKES 8 SERVINGS
AS DESSERT**

Takes about 45 minutes

1 box (14 ounces) refrigerated
unbaked pie crust (top and
bottom crusts)

¾ cup (3 ounces) shredded
sharp cheddar cheese
(optional)

2 large Granny Smith apples

2 large Golden Delicious
apples

Juice of 1 lemon

2 teaspoons cornstarch

½ cup sugar

¼ teaspoon kosher salt

2 teaspoons pure vanilla extract

Whipped cream, for serving

Pie crust can be chips too! Store-bought pie crust works great as the "chip" in this apple pie nacho recipe. I make the pie filling on the stove and pile it on top of the chips, then dive right in! Here in New England, people put cheddar cheese on top of apple pie. I personally don't like that, but if you do, feel free to add it (I've made it optional) and make these an even more perfect nacho mash-up!

1 Preheat the oven to 400°F with a rack in the center position.

2 Unroll the pie crusts. Cut each into 8 wedges, then cut each wedge into 3 smaller triangles. They don't have to be perfect! Transfer the dough triangles to 2 baking sheets.

3 Bake the dough triangles until they turn golden, about 8 minutes. Flip and continue baking until the triangles are browned and sturdy, about 8 minutes more. Remove from the oven and transfer the dough chips to a sheet pan, overlapping them slightly.

4 Sprinkle the cheese (if using) over the chips, distributing it evenly. Bake until melted, about 5 minutes.

5 Meanwhile, core, peel, and chop the apples into 1-inch cubes (as you cut the apples, put the pieces into a large bowl and drizzle some of the lemon juice on top, tossing to coat, to prevent them from browning). Add the cornstarch, sugar, and salt to the apples and stir to coat. Pour the apple mixture into a large frying pan over medium heat and cook, stirring, until the apples are soft and their liquid has reduced and become syrupy, about 15 minutes. Remove from the heat and stir in the vanilla.

6 Spoon the apple mixture over the chips. Top with whipped cream and serve.

STRAWBERRY SHORTCAKE NACHOS

I was already excited to experiment with strawberry shortcake nachos, but when I found out you could buy shortbread in triangle shapes, I started testing the recipe immediately! Adding a little sugar to strawberries is all you need to form the syrupy sauce that coats the shortbread cookies like nacho cheese.

MAKES 4 SERVINGS AS DESSERT

Takes about 35 minutes

2 cups diced strawberries

¼ cup sugar

¼ teaspoon kosher salt

2 packages (about 10 ounces total) shortbread cookies (preferably triangular if you can find them)

2 cups whipped cream

1 Put the strawberries into a medium-size bowl. Top with the sugar and salt and stir to combine. Cover and refrigerate for 30 minutes or up to 4 hours.

2 Pile the shortbread cookies onto a platter. Pour the strawberry mixture over the cookies.

3 Top with the whipped cream and serve.

MIX-AND-MATCH DESSERT NACHOS!

Making dessert nachos is almost like making a sundae without the ice cream: Take some sweet "chips," add a favorite sauce or two, and pile on the toppings (and if you want to add ice cream, too, go for it!). Here is a table to get your ideas flowing. I also recommend the versions pictured on pages 142 and 143, such as Brownies à la Mode 'Chos (brownies as the base, ice cream on top, with sprinkles and whipped cream) or Churrochos (homemade tortilla chips dusted with cinnamon sugar as they come out of the fryer, then drizzled with chocolate sauce).

"CHIPS"	SAUCES	TOPPINGS
• tortilla chips dusted with cinnamon sugar	• chocolate sauce	• M&M's
• cookies	• hot fudge	• sprinkles
• brownies	• caramel sauce	• caramelized banana slices
• Rice Krispies treats	• marshmallow sauce	• sugar cereals (such as Lucky Charms)
• pretzels	• fruit jam	• macerated strawberries
• pizzelles	• whipped cream	• marshmallows
• candy bars	• vanilla icing	• gummy bears
• graham crackers	• crème anglaise	• chocolate/peanut butter/butterscotch chips
• crisp apple slices	• pastry cream	• toasted coconut flakes
• waffle cone pieces	• pudding	• chopped peanuts/almonds/pecans
	• lemon curd	• crushed Oreos
	• warmed jam	• cookie dough bites
		• toffee bits

S'MORES NACHOS

**MAKES 4 SERVINGS
AS DESSERT**

Takes about 15 minutes

1 packet graham crackers
(9 crackers), broken into
18 squares

¾ cup semisweet chocolate
chips

1 cup mini marshmallows

The actual best dessert of all time uses graham crackers, and I wrote a whole book about it. (Hint: It has "s'mores" in the title.) Graham crackers work great as the "chip" in dessert nachos, but they have an odd tendency to melt in the oven, so you have to hit them with high heat for a short period of time. The crackers can burn easily as well—keep an eye on them as they bake.

1 Preheat the oven to 400°F with one rack in the center and another 4 inches from the heat.

2 Arrange the graham crackers in a large shallow cast-iron skillet, being careful not to let the edges hang off too much.

3 Top the grahams with the chocolate and marshmallows, alternating between the two so that the chocolate and marshmallows are evenly combined.

4 Bake on the center rack until the chocolate and marshmallows melt, about 5 minutes. Move the pan to the top rack and turn the oven to broil on low. Broil to brown the marshmallows slightly, about 2 minutes. (Watch carefully to make sure they don't burn.) Remove from the oven. Serve hot.

CONVERSION TABLES

Please note that all conversions are approximate but close enough to be useful when converting from one system to another.

OVEN TEMPERATURES

FAHRENHEIT	GAS MARK	CELSIUS
250	½	120
275	1	140
300	2	150
325	3	160
350	4	180
375	5	190
400	6	200
425	7	220
450	8	230
475	9	240
500	10	260

NOTE: Reduce the temperature by 20°C (68°F) for fan-assisted ovens.

APPROXIMATE EQUIVALENTS

1 stick butter = 8 tbs = 4 oz = ½ cup = 115 g

1 cup all-purpose presifted flour = 4.7 oz

1 cup granulated sugar = 8 oz = 220 g

1 cup (firmly packed) brown sugar = 6 oz = 220 to 230 g

1 cup confectioners' sugar = 4½ oz = 115 g

1 cup honey or syrup = 12 oz = 350 g

1 cup grated cheese = 4 oz = 125 g

1 cup dried beans = 6 oz = 175 g

1 large egg = about 2 oz or about 3 tbs

1 egg yolk = about 1 tbs

1 egg white = about 2 tbs

LIQUID CONVERSIONS

U.S.	IMPERIAL	METRIC
2 tbs	1 fl oz	30 ml
3 tbs	1½ fl oz	45 ml
¼ cup	2 fl oz	60 ml
⅓ cup	2½ fl oz	75 ml
⅓ cup + 1 tbs	3 fl oz	90 ml
⅓ cup + 2 tbs	3½ fl oz	100 ml
½ cup	4 fl oz	125 ml
⅔ cup	5 fl oz	150 ml
¾ cup	6 fl oz	175 ml
¾ cup + 2 tbs	7 fl oz	200 ml
1 cup	8 fl oz	250 ml
1 cup + 2 tbs	9 fl oz	275 ml
1¼ cups	10 fl oz	300 ml
1⅓ cups	11 fl oz	325 ml
1½ cups	12 fl oz	350 ml
1⅔ cups	13 fl oz	375 ml
1¾ cups	14 fl oz	400 ml
1¾ cups + 2 tbs	15 fl oz	450 ml
2 cups (1 pint)	16 fl oz	500 ml
2½ cups	20 fl oz (1 pint)	600 ml
3¾ cups	1½ pints	900 ml
4 cups	1¾ pints	1 liter

WEIGHT CONVERSIONS

US/UK	METRIC	US/UK	METRIC
½ oz	15 g	7 oz	200 g
1 oz	30 g	8 oz	250 g
1½ oz	45 g	9 oz	275 g
2 oz	60 g	10 oz	300 g
2½ oz	75 g	11 oz	325 g
3 oz	90 g	12 oz	350 g
3½ oz	100 g	13 oz	375 g
4 oz	125 g	14 oz	400 g
5 oz	150 g	15 oz	450 g
6 oz	175 g	1 lb	500 g

INDEX